ADJUNCT FACULTY IN COMMUNITY COLLEGES

ADJUNCT FACULTY IN COMMUNITY COLLEGES

An Academic Administrator's Guide to Recruiting, Supporting, and Retaining Great Teachers

DESNA L. WALLIN
University of Georgia

Editor

ANKER PUBLISHING COMPANY, INC.
Bolton, Massachusetts

Adjunct Faculty in Community Colleges
An Academic Administrator's Guide to Recruiting, Supporting, and Retaining Great Teachers

ISBN 1-882982-81-9

Cover design by Frederick Schneider/Grafis
Composition by Dutton & Sherman Design

Anker Publishing Company, Inc.
563 Main Street
P.O. Box 249
Bolton, MA 01740-0249 USA

www.ankerpub.com

Library of Congress Cataloging-in-Publication Data

Adjunct faculty in community colleges : an academic administrator's guide to recruiting, supporting, and retaining great teachers / Desna L. Wallin, editor.
 p. cm.
Includes bibliographical references and index.
 ISBN 1-882982-81-9
 1. College teachers, Part-time—Recruiting—United States—Handbooks, manuals, etc. 2. College teachers, Part-time—Selection and appointment—United States—Handbooks, manuals, etc. 3. Community college teachers—Recruiting—United States—Handbooks, manuals, etc. 4. Community college teachers—Selection and appointment—United States—Handbooks, manuals, etc. 5. Community colleges—United States—Administration—Handbooks, manuals, etc. I. Wallin, Desna L.
 LB2332.72.A34 2005
 378.1'2—dc22   2004018666

Contents

About the Authors

The Editor

Desna L. Wallin is an assistant professor in the Department of Lifelong Education, Administration, and Policy at the University of Georgia. She has more than 25 years of experience in community and technical colleges. She began her career as an adjunct instructor at Lincoln Land Community College. She subsequently became a tenured instructor, served as dean of transfer, general studies, and developmental programs, and as vice president for academic affairs. She accepted the presidency of Clinton Community College in 1989 and served for six years before assuming the presidency of Forsyth Technical Community College, where she served for an additional six years. She is the author of numerous articles and chapters, a coauthor of *Essentialism: Common Sense Quality Improvement* (American Association of Community Colleges, 1994) and author of *The CEO Contract: A Guide for Presidents and Boards* (American Association of Community Colleges, 2003). An active leadership consultant, she is currently working with various state organizations and the American Association of Community Colleges to provide leadership development seminars and workshops for faculty and administrators in community and technical colleges.

Dr. Wallin is an honors graduate of Brigham Young University. She earned her master's degree in English education at Eastern Illinois University and her Ed.D. in curriculum and instruction from Illinois State University. She can be reached at dwallin@uga.edu.

The Contributors

Duane Akroyd is associate professor of higher education administration and director of graduate programs in the Department of Adult and Community College Education at North Carolina State University. He can be reached at duane_akroyd@ncsu.edu.

Thomas I. Anderson is assistant to the president and vice president of instruction at Brookhaven College. He can be reached at txa2482@dcccd.edu.

Helen Burnstad is Director Emeritus of staff and organizational development at Johnson County Community College. She can be reached at helenb@jccc.net.

Amy L. Caison is coordinator for planning and comparative studies in the Department of Adult and Community College Education and University Planning and Analysis at North Carolina State University. She can be reached at amy_caison@ncsu.edu.

Dale F. Campbell is professor and director of the Community College Leadership Consortium at the University of Florida. He can be reached at dfc@coe.ufl.edu.

Hazel M. Davis is faculty chair for library science at Rio Salado College. She can be reached at hazel.davis@riomail.maricopa.edu.

Joseph L. Gadberry is coordinator of the adjunct certification training program and assistant dean of science, health care, and math at Johnson County Community College. He can be reached at jgadber@jccc.net.

Laura Helminski is faculty chair for communication and reading at Rio Salado College. She can be reached at laura.helminski@riomail.maricopa.edu.

Kristina Kauffman is dean of faculty and 4faculty.org project director at Riverside Community College District. She can be reached at kristina.kauffman@rcc.edu.

Richard E. Lyons is senior consultant with Faculty Development Associates. He can be reached at lyons@developfaculty.com.

Eduardo J. Marti is president of Queensborough Community College. He can be reached at emarti@qcc.cuny.edu

Kristel D. Phillips is faculty development consultant and education professor at Valencia Community College. She can be reached at kristelP@aol.com.

Vernon C. Smith is faculty chair for foreign languages at Rio Salado College. He can be reached at vernon.smith@riomail.maricopa.edu

Deborah Stewart is associate academic dean at the Community College of Vermont. She can be reached at stewartd@mail.ccv.vsc.edu.

Alice W. Villadsen is president of Brookhaven College. She can be reached at avilladsen@dccd.edu.

Richard L. Wagoner is at the Center for the Study of Higher Education at the University of Arizona. He can be reached at rwagoner@email.arizona.edu.

Rebecca Werner is associate academic dean of the Community College of Vermont. She can be reached at wernerr@mail.ccv.vsc.edu.

FOREWORD

Community colleges continue a trend of increased utilization of part-time faculty in response to new demands and to uncertainties in funding and enrollment patterns. As this book points out, specialized expertise is a strong motivating factor in the employment of adjunct instructors. It is not always possible in specialty areas to locate full-time faculty with expertise equivalent to that of a part-timer employed in the field. Indeed, in some disciplines, it is impossible to attract full-time employees at prevailing faculty wages.

However, an even stronger motivation may be economic. The exigencies of eroding financial bases on the one hand and extraordinary enrollment pressures and cost increases on the other present college leaders with few alternatives if they are to maximize both access and quality. There is widespread agreement that instruction delivered by part-time faculty costs less than that provided by full-time staff. This economic advantage occurs because part-timers are usually paid on a student-contact hour or course rate rather than on a prorated salary schedule. Some studies have reported part-time faculty compensation rates as low as one-third that of full-timers. Further savings result from minimal expenses for fringe benefits, retirement plans, telephones, office furniture, and travel.

Adjunct professors have also served as a buffer against funding instability. Given their general lack of job security, they are usually the first to go in any retrenchment effort. In this regard, they act to protect the job security of full-time faculty.

Studies of the effectiveness of adjunct faculty have generally shown that they provide high-quality services to community colleges and their students. Research based mainly on student ratings reveals no statistical difference between full-time and part-time faculty. My own dissertation research, in which I tracked students from developmental writing to freshman composition, revealed no statistical difference in the grades that students received in freshman composition whether their teachers in developmental writing were full- or part-time.

Despite these studies of quality, it is also clear that colleges do not often provide the support that they should to adjunct faculty. Selection processes are not as rigorous as they are for full-timers and orientation programs are generally weak. Part-timers often teach at odd hours, off campus, and without direct supervision. All too often, evaluation of their teaching does not occur. Assimilating adjunct faculty into the culture of the college is not seen as important as it should be.

Adjunct Faculty in Community Colleges: An Academic Administrator's Guide to Recruiting, Supporting, and Retaining Great Teachers points out how important hiring, orientation, acculturation, and professional development are for part-time faculty. Their experiences and best practices provide models for our colleges.

Community colleges are human services organizations. We are only as strong as our people. The selection, orientation, evaluation, support, and professional development of all employees are essential processes if we are to assure quality. These processes are as important for adjunct faculty as they are for everyone else at our institutions. Interactions between faculty and students have been shown to be one of the strongest determinants of student success in learning. We need to do the best job that we can of choosing the right people to teach and to provide the support and working conditions students need to be most effective. This book will help community college leaders to improve their institutions by highlighting the importance of adjunct faculty and providing examples of best practices.

George R. Boggs, President and CEO
American Association of Community Colleges

PREFACE

This book is intended to highlight the significance of adjunct faculty in America's community colleges. It is not an exaggeration to say that without the work of adjunct faculty, community colleges could not begin to fulfill their critical teaching mission while maintaining access and affordability. Yet despite their importance to community colleges, adjunct faculty frequently have little or no opportunity for professional development and often lack the basic amenities that are taken for granted by their full-time peers.

It is important to realize that one size does not fit all when it comes to understanding the needs and challenges of adjunct teaching. Some part-time faculty are seeking to cobble together a full-time job by organizing several teaching assignments at different institutions. Some are teaching as a way of giving back to their professions. Often, attorneys, police officers, bankers, and small business owners teach out of a desire to help others become a part of their profession. Still others may be employed outside of education but choose to teach for the satisfaction and intrinsic rewards they experience in dealing with students. But regardless of their reasons for teaching, all need varying degrees of support if the colleges that hire them are to retain this valuable human resource.

The contributors to this volume were selected in a variety of ways. Some were chosen through the extensive writings of practitioners and researchers and the reputation of their colleges. Others were selected on the basis of presentations at professional conferences. Still others were invited on the recommendation of colleagues who were aware of their commitment to adjunct faculty support. While there are only a few colleges whose experiences are delineated in these pages, they are representative of colleges across the country that are making diligent and consistent efforts, even during times of financial challenges, to keep the needs and contributions of adjunct faculty squarely as a front-burner issue.

The book contains 13 chapters organized into three parts. Part One, Understanding Part-Time Faculty, provides introductory material and lays out the characteristics of part-time faculty, the pros and cons of employing part-time faculty, and the recurring issues of instructional quality. Chapter 1 provides the theoretical and conceptual underpinning for the chapters that follow. It details the history and development of adjunct faculty in community colleges and reviews the theories of motivation and adult learning that need to be considered in developing appropriate professional support for adjunct faculty. Chapter 2 provides an overview of part-time faculty and compares them with their full-time counterparts using data from the 1999 National Study of Postsecondary Faculty. The benefits and drawbacks of having a ready corps of adjunct faculty and the issues of quality of instruction are topics discussed in Chapter 3. Chapter 4 continues the exploration of adjunct faculty and quality of instruction coupled with professional development through a review of a survey of Florida Community Colleges.

Part Two, Recruiting and Retaining Part-Time Faculty, explores issues of hiring, orientation, acculturation, and professional development for adjunct faculty. The hiring and orientation of part-time faculty should be considered one of the most important responsibilities of department or division heads. Chapter 5 reviews the experiences of Johnson County Community College in hiring and assimilating adjunct faculty into the teaching and learning environment. Chapter 6 further explores hiring, orientation, and support for adjunct faculty at Brookhaven College. While it is important to hire the right people and to spend the time necessary to properly orient and support them, it is both effective and efficient to be sure that appropriate strategies are developed to retain part-time faculty. In Chapter 7 the experience of Johnson County Community College in creating a campus culture and climate where part-time faculty are valued as a critical component of the institution's mission is detailed. Chapter 8 delineates the initiative of Indian River Community College in launching a comprehensive professional development program focused on the expressed needs of part-time faculty.

Realizing that a majority of part-time faculty are employed full-time in other occupations, many colleges have begun using the technology available through the Internet to support and sustain adjunct faculty. Part Three, Supporting Part-Time Faculty Through Technology, explores various efforts to use online capabilities to provide professional development to adjunct faculty and ends with a summary chapter. Chapter 9 describes 4 faculty.org, a collaboration of California community colleges that have come together to orient adjunct faculty quickly and efficiently through the Internet. Chapter 10 describes the Community College of Vermont (CCV), where part-time instructors teach 100% of the courses. As a result, CCV has developed innovative methods to support their more than 700 adjunct instructors. Rio Salado College is another nontraditional college that employs only 28 permanent residential faculty and nearly 850 adjunct faculty. The college has a deliberate model for recruiting, hiring, training, and supporting adjunct faculty through a systems approach that is described in Chapter 11. Chapter 12 examines the online adjunct training environment at one Florida community college to evaluate its effectiveness and its potential as a model to better integrate part-time faculty into the academic life of a campus. Chapter 13 summarizes the major issues addressed in the previous chapters and provides suggestions and recommendations for community colleges that recognize the importance of their adjunct faculty to the success of their institutions.

The book is not intended to be definitive, but instead to spark ideas and generate commitment for adjunct faculty. The colleges referenced within the book are models of support for adjunct faculty and all are willing to share their successes with other community colleges. Further, there are many other community colleges not represented within these pages that similarly have innovative programs to support their adjunct faculty. Perhaps the experiences shared here will generate a larger network where administrators and faculty can communicate, network, and share ideas to successfully recruit, support, and retain great teachers. The students of America's community colleges deserve no less!

Desna L. Wallin
University of Georgia

ACKNOWLEDGMENTS

The author wishes to acknowledge Dr. Clifton L. Smith of the Department of Workforce Education at the University of Georgia, who recognized the need and encouraged the writing of this book.

PART ONE

*Understanding
Part-Time Faculty*

1 | VALUING AND MOTIVATING PART-TIME FACULTY

Desna L. Wallin

Two-thirds of faculty at public community and technical colleges throughout the country are part-time employees. According to the National Center for Education Statistics (U.S. Department of Education, 1999), 66% of two-year college faculty are part-time/adjunct and 34% are full-time. Merriam-Webster's online dictionary (2004) defines an adjunct as "something joined or added to another thing but not essentially a part of it." However, at nearly two-thirds of all faculty, adjuncts are clearly an essential part of community colleges.

Adjunct or part-time instructors (the terms are used synonymously throughout this book) have been an important part of the instructional staffs of community and technical colleges since the beginning of such institutions. Adjuncts are valued for their specialized knowledge and the real-world experience they can bring to students. They also bring obvious economic benefits to a college inasmuch as adjuncts are usually paid much less than permanent faculty. In most cases, they do not receive fringe benefits, nor do they require office space or secretarial support (Witt, Wattenbarger, Gollattscheck, & Suppiger, 1994). In fact, "because part-time instructors typically have other income sources, the lower pay they accept as secondary income helps community colleges balance their budgets" (Phillippe, 2000, p. 76).

However, while many of these part-time faculty have a great command of their subject matter, they may have little, if any, experience teaching what they know. They are often hired at the last minute to meet a particular area of growth and they may have few resources other than their own knowledge. They may be unfamiliar with textbooks; they may not be comfortable preparing a syllabus; they may not have the expertise to conduct group work or class discussions. Because they are usually employed elsewhere full-time, they may not have the commitment to office hours, curricular development, and a sense of responsibility to the college that is more typical of full-time faculty (Rifkin, 2000).

Further, because of the heavy course load typical of community and technical college faculty, it is difficult for full-time faculty to provide effective mentoring for part-timers. Department heads and deans most often deal with part-time faculty, but they may not have current teaching experience and are preoccupied with other administrative functions. Thus, a major issue for many community colleges across the nation is providing part-time faculty with appropriate support and pedagogical assistance. Colleges have responded to these challenges in a number of ways, some of which are highlighted as best practices in the chapters that follow.

Part-time faculty have indeed become an integral part of the community college landscape. Whether they are viewed positively as bringing a contribution through their connections with business and industry or negatively as taking away slots that should rightfully be held by full-time academics, they are nevertheless here to stay. In fact, as Cohen and Brawer (2003) have emphasized,

> More so than in the universities, less so than in the for-profit sector, community colleges depend on a part-time workforce. The reasons part-timers continue to be employed in sizable numbers are that they cost less; they may have special capabilities not available among the full-time instructors; and they can be employed, dismissed, and reemployed as necessary. (p. 85)

This chapter will consider the value of part-time faculty, recruiting and orienting part-time faculty, and motivating and supporting adjunct faculty.

Understanding and Valuing Adjunct Faculty

Community colleges, much like other areas of the American economy, are increasingly looking to augment their workforce through part-time labor. Wyles (1998) correctly maintains that the

> situation for part-time faculty is simply a microcosm of our national economy in which one in three workers is a contingent worker. Nationally, from 1969–1992 the number of part-time workers has increased by 88.9 percent and approximately 75 percent of new teaching jobs are filled by part-time faculty. . . . The shift to increasing the numbers of part-time hires is part of the wider employment pattern of downsizing, subcontracting, and outsourcing. (p. 90)

Valadez and Antony (2001) indicate that this trend in hiring part-time faculty is likely to continue for several reasons including:

> (a) increases in instruction-related costs relative to revenues; (b) efforts by academic administrators to achieve staffing flexibility; (c) the number of individuals with advanced degrees who have been unable to obtain full-time teaching positions; and (d) the growth of community colleges, which traditionally have employed large percentages of part-time faculty members. (pp. 97–98)

Colleges have come to depend on low-cost labor to balance their budgets. In fact, Cohen and Brawer (2003) maintain that "part-time instructors are to the community colleges as migrant workers are to the farms" (p. 86). As state support declines and there is more competition for the public dollar from Medicare, social security, and other mandated social programs, state legislatures have increasingly turned to higher education, including community colleges, for assistance in trimming the state budgets.

Yet these same part-time faculty can bring to the classroom skills and understandings of the contemporary business climate that full-time faculty, long out of business and industry if ever they were involved, cannot. Thus, in certain niche areas part-time faculty may make it possible for colleges to offer courses that they could not otherwise teach such as law, religion, or languages. However, the down side of the use of part-timers may be "when the college brings in two or more part-timers to teach similar courses as a way of avoiding employing a full-timer, or when they are overrepresented in classes that the full-timers prefer not to teach, such as developmental or those offered at night or on weekends" (Cohen & Brawer, 2003, p. 89).

Despite conventional wisdom to the contrary, most part-time faculty do perform well. Cohen and Brawer suggest that many studies have found that students learn as much in the classes of part-timers and are as likely to be retained as are students taught by full-time faculty. They have no more discipline problems, their student evaluations and the grades they give to students are comparable to those of full-time instructors.

> Still, they occupy a different status. They are chosen less carefully, the rationale being that because the institution is making no long-term commitment to them, there is no need to spend a great deal of time and money in selection. (p. 87)

Yet part-time faculty by their large numbers and the courses they teach have a tremendous influence on the reputation of the colleges. For many students, part-time faculty are the college.

> If good teaching is the hallmark of American community colleges, then colleges should bring serious attention to the critical steps of identifying those who can best deliver it. It is not possible for colleges to spend too much time or effort in choosing the people who have the colleges' reputations in their hands. (Roueche, Roueche, & Milliron, 1995, p. 58)

Motivating and Supporting Part-Time Faculty

"What do elephants and part-time faculty have in common—both work for peanuts," so reads a news release from the American Federation of Teachers (2001). The importance of salary and benefits issues cannot be overestimated. There is more interest from part-time faculty in becoming represented by unions and making their issues clear before state legislatures. Administrators need to be creative and concerned about the financial inequities faced by part-time faculty and attempt to mitigate those concerns through salary schedules, availability of group insurance, and providing some resources for travel and conference attendance for long-serving adjunct faculty. Administrators also should look to professional development opportunities for their part-timers.

But these concerns are not new. Nearly 25 years ago, some of the same ideas were being discussed in the literature. "The vital role played by part-time faculty will withstand the instructional, philosophic, and legal problems. Part-time faculty represent enrichment, diversity, scheduling flexibility, short-term contractual obligations, and a degree of economic savings, but these remain potential until there are functioning recruitment and retention models" (Harris, 1980, p. 15). Harris goes on to say that often colleges fail to make the most of the diversity and expertise offered by part-time faculty because of the lack of appropriate and well-implemented staff development programs. He maintains that such programs should be mandatory and stipulated by contract, realizing that they provide "a program critical to the successful functioning of the part-time faculty member" (p. 15). Harris further describes the responsibilities of management to recruit, evaluate, and retain part-time faculty members and suggests that one way to attract quality faculty and to retain them is through a strong staff development program that is tailored to the specific needs of part-time faculty. They need to understand what the institution expects of them, as well as how the institution will support them and that information should be specifically stated in contracts or letters of agreement. Through a clear understanding of expectations on both sides, part-time faculty will be regarded as the valuable institutional resources that they are.

Wyles (1998) concurs and makes the case that "integrating adjunct faculty into the culture of the learning organization becomes a critical goal for higher education institutions" (p. 92). If this is not effectively done, she maintains, part-time faculty will simply remain faculty of convenience, without any real say in their working conditions and disconnected from the community of learners.

Part-time faculty mirror dramatic changes in the wider world of work in which there are fewer definitive jobs and more temporary "work situations." In these ways, higher education has come to depend on part-time faculty to reinvent itself in a time of great change. We cannot afford to marginalize such an important part of our faculty. (p. 92)

So how do community college leaders go about supporting and sustaining great teachers? What is it that motivates part-time faculty? How can administrators design professional development and other support programs that take into account the skills, abilities, and knowledge that the adjunct faculty member already possesses?

Part-time faculty are motivated to teach for a number of reasons.

Their reasons for teaching are as diverse as the students they serve. Some see adjunct teaching as a possible entry to a full-time faculty position. Some are merely trying to bring in a little extra money. Some—attorneys, business people, police officers—are teaching as a service and a way to give back to the community that supports them. Others, such as nurses and allied health professionals, have a much-needed skill to share. Secondary teachers may like the challenge and change of working with adults. Still others teach because they like being on a college campus. (Wallin, 2004, p. 2)

Realizing that part-timers teach for a variety of reasons, administrators need to ask themselves how they can best support these valued employees, integrate them into the culture of the institution, and become a part of the learning community that is the community college. Community college administrators are often concerned that faculty understand that they are teaching adult students with a variety of needs, backgrounds, and abilities. However, they often do not bring that same thinking when planning and organizing professional development experiences for part-time faculty.

An understanding of the ways in which adults learn is essential to implementing successful professional development for adjunct faculty. More than 30 years ago, Malcolm Knowles proposed a distinction between adult learning and pre-adult learning. He used the term "andragogy," meaning the art and science of helping adults learn as contrasted with the more familiar "pedagogy," the art and science of helping children learn. Adragogy is based on five assumptions that are essential to understanding the adult learner.

1) As a person matures, self-concept moves from dependency to self-direction.
2) Adults accumulate experience, which is a rich resource for learning.
3) An adult's readiness to learn is closely linked to his or her social role.
4) Adult learners are more problem centered than subject centered.
5) Adults are motivated more by internal factors than by external factors.

From these five assumptions, "Knowles drew numerous implications for the design, implementation, and evaluation of learning activities with adults" (Merriam & Caffarella, 1999, p. 272). These implications included the climate for learning, which he felt needed to be one that gave adults acceptance and respect and the sense of "adultness" in the organization and physical space in the classroom. He also believed that because adults have the capability to be self-directing, they should participate more fully in the planning, implementation, and evaluation of their learning experiences.

While Knowles's model is the most familiar, there are other, more contemporary models for adult learning that are applicable to providing professional development experiences for part-time faculty. Knox's proficiency theory emphasizes the gap between what adults currently know and what they want to be able to do or to know. In the late 1980s, transformational learning came to the forefront of adult learning. Unlike andragogy and various forms of self-directed learning, transformational learning emphasizes change—"dramatic, fundamental change in the way we see ourselves and the world in which we live" (Merriam & Caffarella, 1999, p. 318). Transformative learning is more than just adding information and improving performance. Experience, inner meaning, and reflection all play a major role in transformational learning. "That the outcome of transformational learning is development is congruent with the growth orientation of much of adult learning literature" (Merriam & Caffarella, 1999, pp. 331–332). Thus, "learning in adulthood can be distinguished from childhood in terms of the learner, the context, and to some extent the learning process" (p. 389).

Hansman (2001) discusses further the importance of context in adult learning.

> The core idea in situated cognition is that learning is inherently social in nature. The nature of the interactions among learners, the tools they use within these interactions, the activity itself, and the social context in which the activity takes place shape learning. . . . From a situated view, people learn as they participate and become intimately involved with a community or culture of learning, interacting with the community and learning to understand and participate in its history, assumptions, and cultural values and rules. . . . These ideas of learning from more experienced members of a community and participation in cultures of practice have lead to a number of concepts of planning and managing learning situations that can incorporate situated views of learning. (pp. 45–46)

It is easy to see the potential application of these theories/concepts to the preparation of professional development programs which truly involve learning, critical thinking, transformation, and active participation, whether that participation is face-to-face or as is increasingly the case, online participation. "Viewing knowledge and learning through this lens allows adult educators and program planners to create or enhance contexts for adult learning that allow learners to share in the design, process, and evaluation of their learning activities" (p. 49). The professional development activities that are highlighted in subsequent chapters all share an understanding of the ways in which adults learn and what is necessary in involving, motivating, and supporting activities that embrace learning in a meaningful context for adjunct faculty.

In addition to having an understanding of how adults best learn, it is also requisite to the planning of professional development activities to understand what motivates part-time faculty. Motivation can be defined as the "willingness to do something . . . conditioned by this action's ability to satisfy some need for the individual" (Robbins, 2003, p. 43). That need can be physiological, sociological, or psychological. It can be intrinsic or extrinsic. For an adjunct faculty member, the motivation to teach may be physiological and basic—the need to put food on the table. It may be sociological—the need to be a part of a group of kindred spirits. Or it may be psychological—the need to make use of innate abilities and knowledge and the desire to share that knowledge.

Abraham Maslow's hierarchy of needs theory is probably the most familiar of classical motivational theories. His five needs are well-known to everyone who has taken an introductory psychology course.

1) Physiological needs
2) Safety needs
3) Social needs
4) Esteem needs
5) Self-actualization needs

While there is little empirical research to back up his theory, it is relatively intuitive and easy to understand. People can identify with the hierarchy of needs and can use the theory in attempting to motivate and bring out the best in their faculty.

Another well-known theory of motivation that can be applied to part-time faculty is that of Frederick Herzberg. He believed that one's attitude toward work can be the determining factor in whether or not one is successful. In his studies, he found that

> intrinsic factors, such as advancement, recognition, responsibility, and achievement seem to be related to job satisfaction. Respondents who felt good about their work tended to attribute these factors to themselves. On the other hand, dissatisfied respondents tended to cite extrinsic factors, such as supervision, pay, company policies, and working conditions. (Robbins, 2003, p. 47)

He found that the opposite of job satisfaction is not job dissatisfaction; in fact, when some of the extrinsic factors such as low pay and less than satisfactory working conditions were removed, employees could still be dissatisfied. Herzberg suggested that other factors associated with the work itself were what made employees satisfied: "opportunities for personal growth, recognition, responsibility, and achievement" (p. 46). In other words, it was the intrinsic reward that motivated individuals. Thus, the often repeated comments of community college part-time faculty that they do what they do for the love of teaching or for the contribution to the community and not for the money makes sense taken in the context of Herzberg's two-factor theory of motivation. Administrators would do well to provide opportunities for personal growth and recognition of part-time faculty.

More recent theories of motivation relate to contemporary adjunct faculty as well. For example, goal-setting theory suggests that intentions can be a major source of work motivation. Adjunct faculty who are able to participate in establishing goals for a course or for a department may develop greater buy-in and commitment to the enterprise.

Perhaps one of the strongest and most comprehensive of motivational theories is that known as expectancy theory.

> Expectancy theory argues that the strength of a tendency to act in a certain way depends on the strength of an expectation that the act will be followed by a given outcome and on the attractiveness of that outcome to the individual. . . . Whether one has the desire to produce at any given time depends on one's particular goals and one's perception of the relative worth of performance as a path to the attainment of those goals. (Robbins, 2003, p. 52)

Vroom (1964) defines an expectancy as a "belief concerning the likelihood that a particular act will be followed by a particular outcome" (p. 17). For example, if an adjunct faculty member believes that an excellent performance in the classroom will potentially open the door to the possibility of full-time employment, and full-time employment at the college is a goal, that faculty member will be motivated to put forth extra effort to perform at the highest possible level. Expectancy theory emphasizes positive payoffs—good performance is rewarded. Where such opportunities are available, for example, where colleges frequently hire their part-time faculty who have proven themselves to be effective teachers into full-time jobs, expectancy theory can be a powerful motivator.

Summary and Conclusions

Clearly, adjunct faculty contribute significantly to the success of community colleges. They make it possible to meet the increasing demands for higher education and workforce development. They bring specialized skills and flexible working hours. Yet they are frequently treated as disposable commodities, an expendable contingent work force. Much more attention needs to be focused on recruiting, orienting, motivating, and supporting part-time faculty. Finally, part-time faculty need to be fully integrated into the culture and life of the college and given appropriate opportunities for professional development. Far from second-class citizens, adjunct faculty in community colleges should be valued and appreciated as professional colleagues.

References

American Federation of Teachers. (2001, October 22). *College and university faculty to hold nationwide protest Oct. 28–Nov. 3 over pay and treatment of adjunct professors.* Washington, DC: Author. Retrieved June 4, 2004, from http://www.aft.org/press/2001/102201_equity.html

Cohen, A. M., & Brawer, F. B. (2003). *The American community college* (4th ed.). San Francisco, CA: Jossey-Bass.

Hansman, C. A. (2001). Context-based adult learning. In S. B. Merriam (Ed.), *New directions for adult and continuing education: No. 89. The new update on adult learning theory* (pp. 43–52). San Francisco, CA: Jossey-Bass.

Harris, D. A. (1980). From the president's perspective: Using part-time faculty effectively. In C. E. Blocker (Ed.), *New directions for community colleges: No. 8. Humanizing student services* (pp. 13–16). San Francisco, CA: Jossey-Bass.

Merriam, S. B., & Caffarella, R. S. (1999). *Learning in adulthood* (2nd ed.). San Francisco, CA: Jossey-Bass.

Merriam-Webster Online. (2004). Retrieved June 1, 2003, from http://
www.m-w.com/cgi-bin/dictionary?book=Dictionary&va=adjunct

Phillippe, K. (Ed.). (2000). *National profile of community colleges: Trends
and statistics* (3rd ed.). Washington, DC: Community College Press.

Rifkin, T. (2000). *Public community college faculty* (New Expeditions
Issues Paper No. 4). Washington, DC: Community College Press.

Robbins, S. P. (2003). *Essentials of organizational behavior* (7th ed.).
Upper Saddle River, NJ: Prentice Hall.

Roueche, J. E., Roueche, S. D., & Milliron, M. D. (1995). *Strangers
in their own land: Part-time faculty in American community colleges.*
Washington, DC: Community College Press.

U.S. Department of Education, National Center for Education
Statistics. (1999). *Integrated postsecondary education data system fall
staff survey.* Washington, DC: Author.

Valadez, J. R., & Antony, J. S. (2001). Job satisfaction and commitment of two-year college part-time faculty. *Community College
Journal of Research and Practice, 25,* 97–108.

Vroom, V. H. (1964). *Work and motivation.* New York, NY: John
Wiley & Sons.

Wallin, D. L. (2004). Valuing professional colleagues: Adjunct faculty
in community and technical colleges. *Community College Journal of
Research and Practice, 28,* 1–19.

Witt, A., Wattenbarger, J., Gollattscheck, J., & Suppiger, J. (1994).
America's community colleges. Washington, DC: Community
College Press.

Wyles, B. (1998). Adjunct faculty in the community college: Realities
and challenges. In D. W. Leslie (Ed.), *New directions for higher education: No. 104. The growing use of part-time faculty: Understanding
causes and effects* (pp. 89–93). San Francisco, CA: Jossey-Bass.

2 | Part-Time Community College Faculty and Their Full-Time Counterparts

Duane Akroyd and Amy L. Caison

Research has established that part-time faculty comprise a substantial portion of higher education faculty and constitute the majority among community college instructors (Conley, Leslie, & Zimbler, 2002). The National Center for Educational Statistics (NCES) estimated that in 1988, 52% of all community college faculty were part-time, and in 1993 this majority grew to 60% (U.S. Department of Education, 1997). With decreasing budgets and increasing demand for more course sections, community colleges are often forced to break up the funds for one full-time faculty position and create several part-time contract positions which can be taught by multiple faculty of various specializations (Pollack, 1986). This change has left a large portion of faculty in a marginalized circumstance where compensation, collegial esteem, and benefits are greatly reduced or even absent (Pratt, 1997). Despite calls for reform, academic administrations are hard pressed to find a more workable solution to financial pressures and shifting course demands. Indeed, Pratt reports that the percentage of part-time faculty is more than twice that of part-time workers in the overall U.S. workforce and is projected to continue to increase in the coming years.

As a growing majority in community colleges, researchers have worked hard to study part-time faculty in order to better understand key demographic and attitudinal facets of this important group (e.g.,

Conley et al., 2002). This understanding is vital if community colleges are to effectively utilize part-time faculty to maintain a vibrant and effective learning environment. A central tool employed in this effort has been the National Study of Postsecondary Faculty (NSOPF), which is administered by the National Center for Education Statistics and explores the demographics, attitudes, and opinions of faculty in all institutional types in the U.S. The NSOPF is a recurring study conducted in 1988, 1993, and, most recently, 1999. Research based on these and other national, regional, and institutional surveys have focused on studies of faculty demographics, satisfaction, instructional practices, integration, and educational costs of faculty.

Literature Review

In studying part-time faculty, it is essential to contextualize the findings by including full-time faculty in the analysis as a comparison group. This approach is important because, though part-time faculty are the dominant group among two-year colleges, higher education faculty have traditionally been hired in a full-time status, and deviations from a historical pattern can indicate critical issues for community college administrations. As the makeup of community colleges changes in response to environmental forces, administrations must understand the impact of these changes if their institutions are to excel.

Following this pattern, the comprehensive report by Conley et al. (2002) employed the 1993 NSOPF to explore in greater detail the characteristics of part-time faculty, the nature of their activities, and how they feel about what they do in relation to full-time instructional faculty. Results from this study indicate that part-time faculty are more likely to be female and that part-time faculty feel they have less institutional support and report different motivations for teaching than full-time faculty. In addition, nearly one half (49%) of part-time faculty hold a full-time job in addition to their community college teaching responsibilities. The analysis also explores part-time faculty perceptions of the availability of instructional resources, job satisfaction, and campus trends. While offering a broad survey of issues pertinent to part-time faculty and juxtaposing these findings against the characteristics and attitudes of full-time faculty, this report often collapses faculty from both two- and four-year institutions, which precludes a detailed analysis of part-time faculty in the community college.

Keim (1989) conducted a national study of full- and part-time faculty in two-year colleges using a specially designed instrument which addressed class size, teaching style and effectiveness, scholarly activity, and numerous demographic factors. The study indicated that part-time faculty outnumbered full-time faculty and that the part-time faculty lagged behind full-time faculty in terms of experience, academic preparation, and job satisfaction.

Employing a national survey conducted by the Center for the Study of Community Colleges as a supplement to the 1993 NSOPF dataset, Leslie and Gappa (2002) explored both full- and part-time faculty in two-year colleges. This study also produced a comprehensive profile of community college faculty in terms of employment status, finding that part-timers resemble full-timers in many ways (e.g., interests, attitudes, and motives). A notable finding of this study contradicts the popularly held belief that faculty prefer full-time employment and only take part-time positions because full-time positions are not available. In fact, Leslie and Gappa found that just over half (51%) of part-time faculty prefer to teach part-time.

Using the 1988 and 1999 NSOPF datasets, Liu, Finkelstein, and Schuster (2002) concentrated on exploring how the profile of only part-time instructional faculty has changed over time. Their analysis shows that the use of part-time faculty has increased from the first NSOPF to the third NSOPF administration in 1999. They highlight the diversity among part-timers though their study population included all institutional types, which limits the ability of this research to contribute meaningfully to the understanding of the circumstances of part-time community college faculty.

A recent study by Antony and Valadez (2002) employed the 1993 NSOPF data to explore satisfaction and commitment for a national sample of part-time faculty by institutional type (i.e., two-year and four-year institutions). While they found no differences in satisfaction between part-time faculty at two-year institutions and part-time faculty at four-year institutions, they did not compare full-time and part-time faculty views of their work within two-year institutions. Information on faculty differences in satisfaction and commitment by institutional type (two year versus four year) is helpful, but given differences in institutional mission and goals, it would be useful to examine such workplace issues between faculty groups (full-time and part-time) within the same institutional setting (i.e., only two-year colleges). Community colleges may be better able to address issues related to faculty work when comparative data for faculty groups are examined.

Truell, Price, and Joyner (1998) utilize the Wood's Faculty Satisfaction/Dissatisfaction Scale to explore job satisfaction among community college occupational-technical faculty. Notably, this study compared the satisfaction of both full- and part-time faculty on 10 satisfaction factors. Results concurred with Anthony and Valadez (2002) in finding that both faculty groups were, overall, satisfied with their jobs.

Schuetz (2002) explored differences in instructional practices of part-time and full-time faculty using the 2000 Center for the Study of Community Colleges (CSCC) national faculty survey. Results indicated that differences do exist between full- and part-time community college faculty on matters pertaining to student instruction. Schuetz argues that part-timers interact with students, peers, and their institutions less than their full-time counterparts. Part-time faculty were found to interact with students outside of the classroom to a lesser degree than full-time faculty, which suggests that part-time faculty offer a lesser academic experience as this sort of faculty-student interaction has been documented to improve student outcomes (Endo & Harpel, 1982; Pascarella, 1980; Pascarella & Terenzini, 1977).

Erwin and Andrews (1993) examined 283 Midwestern community colleges and found that many of these institutions were actively working to assist part-time faculty to improve their instructional skills, though there appears to be little effort among these institutions to actively integrate these faculty into their institutional culture in other capacities. Exacerbating this problem is a very limited commitment to merit recognition of part-time faculty, most likely because 41% of these institutions had a poor evaluation system for these faculty.

Roueche, Roueche, and Milliron (1996) qualitatively explored the utilization and integration of part-time community college faculty. Results suggest that community colleges must take steps to integrate this faculty group more effectively into the institutional culture. Roueche et al. argue that community colleges should improve recruitment, selection, and hiring practices of part-time faculty and require part-time faculty to participate in institutional orientation and professional development activities during their employment. Further, the authors echo Erwin and Andrews (1993) in their call for improved evaluation of job performance and equitable pay for part-time faculty.

This body of research has demonstrated that the makeup of community college faculty is dynamic, with an ever-increasing number of new faculty hired in a part-time capacity. These new faculty bring diverse opinions and capabilities to the faculty profession, and this evolving faculty landscape demands continued study to document the changing facets of this key group in relation to full-time community college faculty. This is an important task as we argue that in developing any initiatives to improve the climate for community college faculty, contemporaneous comparative examinations of workplace variables between part-time and full-time groups are needed. To that end, this chapter will utilize the 1999 National Study of Postsecondary Faculty (NSOPF-99) to explore the nature and perceptions of public community college faculty and their work in the classroom from the perspective of employment status.

Method

The data used for this study are from the restricted-use NSOPF-99, a survey project funded by NCES (U.S. Department of Education, 2002). It used a three-stage, stratified, clustered probability design to select the sample. The first stage consisted of sampling postsecondary institutions, and the second stage consisted of sampling faculty from first stage institutions. The third stage of sampling consisted of a subsample of nonrespondents to whom intensive follow-up efforts were directed in order to increase the survey response rate. The final dataset consisted of responses from a representative sample of 19,213 faculty working full-time or part-time from a diverse pool of 819 postsecondary educational institutions. There were 8,646 public two-year college faculty respondents from 298 public two-year colleges. The analysis population for this study was determined by selection of all respondents who were employed in a public, two-year institution and who had primary instructional duties in the fall 1998 academic term and taught at least one course for credit in that semester. These criteria resulted in a sample for analysis of 4,434 respondents, 2,130 (48%) who identified as part-time faculty and 2,304 (52%) who identified as full-time faculty. Analysis included cross-tabulations and independent sample t-tests to profile part-time community college faculty and statistically compare them to their full-time counterparts. Cohen's (1988) D statistic was calculated to determine the effect size of significant t-tests.

The literature on part-time faculty has relied on a variety of population definitions and analytical designs. Some of these studies look only at part-time faculty (e.g., Roueche et al., 1996; Schuetz, 2002; Truell et al., 1998) in the community college, which lacks a comparison to the characteristics of full-time faculty. Other studies contextualize their study of part-time faculty by juxtaposing their finding against comparable measures for full-time faculty in either two- and four-year institutions (e.g., Conley et al., 2002) or only among two-year institutions (e.g., Schuetz, 2002; Leslie & Gappa, 2002). The choice of population in these studies is critical as the population determines the usefulness and applicability of the study results. A limitation of these studies centers on the fact that most of the literature on faculty provides little explanation of the analysis population and the rationale behind these decisions. Antony and Valadez (2002) merely note that their analysis population was comprised of NSOPF records where the respondent indicated that teaching was their primary responsibility. Certainly, this group may include administrators and those who teach only non-credit courses, especially those in two-year institutions. This broader population definition can potentially lead to inaccurate conclusions about the core instructional faculty at two-year institutions. Therefore, in this study we adopt a relatively strict definition of faculty to ensure our findings provide a very clear picture of the core faculty in the community college who are working on a daily basis with students. To that end, we have selected only those respondents who 1) identified as working in a public two-year institution, 2) had instructional duties in the fall 1998 semester, 3) taught at least some courses for credit only during the fall 1998 semester, and 4) whose primary responsibility was teaching.

The NSOPF employs a complex sampling design in which oversampling of some groups with certain desirable demographic characteristics ensures adequate representation of these groups. As a result, it is important to take this factor into consideration when analyzing data as the use of unequal probabilities of selection may result in a dataset that is not directly representative of the population (Thomas & Heck, 2001). However, the use of sampling weights corrects for these unequal probabilities of selection and ensures that the sample is representative. The sampling weight determines how many faculty are represented by each respondent in the dataset. Therefore, this analysis utilized sampling weights to ensure that results can be generalized to the national faculty population. Additional technical information about the NSOPF-99 sampling design and weighting methods can be found in the survey's methodology report (U.S. Department of Education, 2002). As noted earlier, the unweighted dataset contained 48% part-time faculty and 52% full-time faculty. However, when the sampling weights are applied to the dataset, 63% are part-time faculty and 37% are full-time faculty, a ratio that is substantiated in the literature on part-time community college faculty. We used cross-tabulations and variable means to explore various demographic and attitudinal differences in full- and part-time faculty. For a comparison of means between faculty groups, *t*-tests were conducted to determine whether a significant difference (alpha = .05) existed between full- and part-time faculty regarding a variable. Where significance was found, Cohen's D was calculated to estimate the effect size of the difference. Qualitative descriptors of a small, medium, or large effect for the absolute value of the Cohen's (1988) D statistic were applied using Cohen's guidelines. Therefore, Cohen's D statistics less than 0.4 are considered small effects. Values of 0.4 to 0.79 are considered medium effects while Cohen's D statistics of 0.8 or greater are classified as large effects.

Results

Any comprehensive analysis of part-time faculty must be accomplished within the context of full-time community college faculty. This is necessary to provide a frame of reference for understanding the unique condition of part-time faculty. In the results that follow, various faculty characteristics are presented according to faculty status. Each contingency table presents both weighted row and weighted column percents to allow for a more complete understanding of the profile of part-time community college faculty. In addition, the NSOPF asks a variety of attitude, satisfaction, and opinion items which were utilized in an in-depth analysis of part-time faculty according to variables such as gender, tenure status, and institutional type.

Faculty Profile

Demographics. Approximately 63% of faculty at public community colleges are employed part-time and 37% work full-time. Part-time faculty were an average of 47.7 years old when they completed the survey in 1999, while their full-time counterparts averaged 49.5 years of age. Men comprised the majority of public two-year college faculty with 55% of part-time faculty identifying as male and 45% as female. Among full-time faculty, 53% were male and 47% were female. Respondents who identified as white comprised the majority of both part-time and full-time faculty in the community college (88% and 86%, respectively). A similar pattern emerges across other races as the percentages of part-time faculty are very similar to the percentages of full-time faculty. In addition, no substantive difference between marital status according to employment status was observed (see Table 2.1). Of those who were either married or who were living with a significant other in a marriage-like relationship, 10% of the part-time faculty spouses were also employed in higher education while 15% of the full-time faculty spouses were employed in higher education.

Academic qualifications. Over three quarters of the public two-year college faculty hold at least a master's degree (76%), with 12.4% of this group holding a doctorate. Three percent (3%) of the faculty do not hold at least an associate's degree, yet they did teach courses for credit

TABLE 2.1
FACULTY DEMOGRAPHICS BY EMPLOYMENT STATUS

Demographics	Part-Time Row % (Column %)		Full-Time Row % (Column %)	
Age				
Under 30	82.71	(3.63)	17.29	(1.31)
30–44	68.74	(33.78)	31.26	(26.57)
45–54	61.89	(37.88)	38.11	(40.35)
55–59	50.54	(11.38)	59.46	(19.26)
60–64	56.91	(6.87)	43.09	(8.99)
65+	76.10	(6.47)	23.90	(3.51)
Gender				
Male	64.36	(54.85)	35.64	(52.54)
Female	62.21	(45.15)	37.79	(47.46)
Marital Status				
Single, never married	67.02	(11.13)	32.98	(9.47)
Married	62.91	(72.21)	37.09	(73.66)
Living with someone	54.56	(1.48)	45.44	(2.13)
Separated, divorced, or widowed	64.07	(15.18)	35.93	(14.73)
Race				
American Indian/Alaska Native	52.54	(0.33)	47.46	(0.52)
Asian/Pacific Islander	51.16	(1.68)	48.84	(2.77)
Black (Non-Hispanic)	62.27	(5.21)	37.73	(5.46)
Hispanic (White or Black)	58.84	(3.73)	41.16	(4.51)
White	63.92	(88.06)	36.08	(86.00)
More than one race/ethnicity	70.19	(0.99)	29.81	(0.73)

Note: % represents weighted percentages.

in the fall 1998 term. A greater proportion of full-time faculty hold doctorates. Notably, part-time faculty outnumber full-time faculty among those who hold a first professional degree, suggesting these professionals supplement their income through community college teaching. Table 2.2 presents a summary of this data.

Employment characteristics. As would be expected, the overwhelming majority (98%) of full-time faculty consider their employment to be their primary job, while 28% of part-timers considered their current position their primary employment. Full-time faculty have typically not retired from another position (96%), which is also the case with part-time faculty, though there is a greater proportion of retired part-time faculty (14%) than full-time faculty (4%). The majority of part-time faculty (62.74) were either not eligible to join a union or union membership was unavailable at their institution, while the majority of full-time faculty did hold a union membership. The average total income earned by part-time faculty was $9,976 and the average salary full-time faculty earned was $48,353 (see Table 2.3). The average number of higher education positions held by part-time faculty (including their present position) was 2.01, while full-time faculty averaged 2.07, suggesting employment status is not related to higher education experience.

A majority of both full- and part-time faculty hold faculty status, though the vast majority of those without faculty status are part-timers. A similar pattern is found regarding the type of appointment held by faculty. Nearly 92% of full-time faculty have a regular appointment while 62% of part-time faculty have a temporary appointment. Tenure status varies widely among full- and part-time faculty, with most tenured faculty employed full-time and most nontenure-track faculty employed part-time. Professorial ranks (i.e., full professor, associate professor, and assistant professor) were dominated by full-time faculty while instructor, lecturer, and other ranks were predominately part-time faculty. Just over half of part-time two-year college faculty teach occupational education courses (53%), with 47% teaching full-time. This division is more substantial in general education courses where 66% are part-time faculty and 34% are full-time. Academic administrative responsibilities are also linked to employment status, with 12% of full-time faculty chairing their department while less than 2% of part-

TABLE 2.2

FACULTY ACADEMIC QUALIFICATIONS BY EMPLOYMENT STATUS

	Part-Time Row % (Column %)	Full-Time Row % (Column %)
Highest Degree Held		
Doctorate	45.92 (8.99)	54.08 (18.32)
First professional	71.37 (2.92)	28.63 (2.02)
Master's	63.36 (60.99)	36.64 (61.00)
Bachelor's	70.07 (17.76)	29.93 (13.12)
Associate's	74.93 (5.37)	25.07 (3.11)
Less than an associate's degree	77.66 (1.77)	22.34 (0.88)
No postsecondary degree or award	71.32 (2.21)	28.68 (1.53)
Working Toward a Degree		
Yes	68.55 (17.33)	31.45 (13.75)
No	62.38 (82.67)	37.62 (86.25)
What Type of Degree Are You Pursuing?		
First professional	74.45 (1.69)	25.55 (1.27)
Doctorate	71.06 (43.98)	28.94 (39.04)
MFA, MSW	54.44 (4.19)	45.56 (7.64)
Other master's	69.90 (35.55)	30.10 (33.36)
Bachelor's	63.61 (10.41)	36.39 (12.98)
Associate's	66.29 (4.02)	33.71 (4.46)
Certificate or diploma	22.56 (0.17)	77.44 (1.26)

Note: % represents weighted percentages.

TABLE 2.3
FACULTY EMPLOYMENT CIRCUMSTANCES BY EMPLOYMENT STATUS

Employment Circumstances	Part-Time Row % (Column %)	Full-Time Row % (Column %)
Current Position Is Primary Employment		
Yes	33.19 (28.06)	66.81 (97.71)
No	98.20 (71.94)	1.80 (2.29)
Retired From Another Position		
Yes	85.40 (13.65)	14.60 (4.04)
No	60.89 (86.35)	39.11 (95.96)
Union Membership		
Yes	41.03 (21.13)	58.97 (52.54)
No	65.26 (16.13)	34.74 (14.86)
Not eligible or not available	76.90 (62.74)	23.10 (32.60)
Salary (total income from institution)		
$5,000 or less	98.71 (43.18)	1.29 (0.97)
$5,001–$15,000	98.53 (41.60)	1.47 (1.07)
$15,001–$38,000	43.71 (11.81)	56.29 (26.32)
$38,001–$51,350	8.37 (1.92)	91.63 (36.45)
$51,350 or more	6.81 (1.49)	93.19 (35.18)

Note: % represents weighted percentages.

timers do so (see Table 2.4). Among part-time faculty, 71% preferred part-time employment and 63% indicated that they were employed part-time because full-time employment was unavailable. An analysis of regional distribution (according to the Bureau of Economic Analysis regional affiliations), institutional size (based on total undergraduate enrollment), and student-faculty ratio of full- and part-time faculty reveals no discernable patterns (see Table 2.5).

TABLE 2.4
FACULTY POSITION CHARACTERISTICS BY EMPLOYMENT STATUS

Faculty Characteristics	Part-Time Row % (Column %)	Full-Time Row % (Column %)
Faculty Status		
Yes	58.85 (81.94)	41.15 (99.13)
No	97.29 (18.06)	2.71 (0.87)
Appointment Type		
Regular	41.77 (38.14)	58.23 (91.98)
Temporary	93.03 (61.86)	6.97 (8.02)
Tenure Status		
Tenured	5.71 (1.87)	94.29 (53.29)
Tenure track, not tenured	16.41 (1.81)	83.59 (15.96)
Not on tenure track, but institution has tenure system	96.20 (71.55)	3.80 (4.89)
No tenure system at this institution	62.37 (24.77)	37.63 (25.86)
Faculty Rank		
Full professor	28.96 (5.47)	71.04 (23.21)
Associate professor	20.34 (1.83)	79.66 (12.37)
Assistant professor	17.68 (1.41)	82.32 (11.38)
Instructor	73.85 (67.64)	26.15 (41.43)
Lecturer	93.34 (4.15)	6.66 (0.51)
Other rank	92.19 (14.04)	7.09 (1.85)
No rank	50.54 (5.46)	49.46 (9.24)
Chair of Department		
Yes	20.41 (1.79)	79.59 (12.08)
No	65.90 (98.21)	34.10 (87.92)
Teaching Discipline		
Occupational education	53.13 (18.71)	46.86 (28.08)
General education	65.80 (81.29)	34.20 (71.92)

Note: % represents weighted percentages.

TABLE 2.5
INSTITUTIONAL CHARACTERISTICS BY EMPLOYMENT STATUS

Institutional Characteristics	Part-Time Row % (Column %)		Full-Time Row % (Column %)	
Bureau of Economic Analysis Region Code				
New England	60.66	(2.51)	39.34	(2.81)
Mideast	58.57	(8.63)	41.43	(10.55)
Great Lakes	65.25	(17.59)	34.75	(16.21)
Plains	58.75	(7.51)	41.25	(9.12)
Southeast	59.25	(19.48)	40.75	(23.18)
Southwest	64.00	(14.96)	36.00	(14.56)
Rocky Mountain	72.39	(6.31)	27.61	(4.17)
Far West	67.77	(22.30)	32.23	(18.35)
Total Institutional Undergraduate Enrollment				
2,538 students or less	54.35	(15.62)	45.65	(22.69)
2,539–4,708 students	61.49	(19.55)	38.51	(21.18)
4,709–8,008 students	63.36	(20.22)	36.64	(20.23)
8,009–14,085 students	67.09	(22.99)	32.91	(19.51)
14,086 students or more	69.54	(21.62)	30.46	(16.39)
Student-Faculty Ratio				
10.0 or less	61.73	(16.52)	38.27	(17.71)
10.1–13.7	63.43	(20.51)	36.57	(20.46)
13.8–16.6	60.48	(18.91)	39.52	(21.38)
16.7–20.7	61.28	(19.24)	38.72	(21.03)
20.8 or more	68.86	(24.82)	31.14	(19.42)

Note: % represents weighted percentages.

Technology. Results of this analysis indicate that there is little difference between full- and part-time instructors in the use of web sites to support instruction; however, among those who use email to communicate with students, a greater proportion of part-time faculty employ this tool than do full-time faculty. Overwhelmingly, both full- and part-time faculty report that less than 20% of their students use email to communicate with them, suggesting that this mode of technology has not substantively penetrated the two-year college (see Table 2.6).

Principle activities. Respondents were asked to estimate the number of hours they spent on a variety of common faculty activities. Independent sample *t*-tests indicate a significant difference between the activities of full- and part-time faculty with regard to several of the activity measures. When found to be significant ($p< 0.05$), Cohen's D statistics were calculated to determine the effect size of this difference. Following Cohen's typology of effect sizes, a medium effect was identified for the average hours faculty spend per week providing individual instruction to undergraduates, with full-time faculty spending an average of 4.6 hours and part-time faculty spending 2.2 hours per week. Large effects were found for the difference between full- and part-time faculty in average total office hours spent each week, average number of hours spent per week on committee work, and average total hours worked per week. No significant difference was found between full- and part-time faculty for the average hours per week spent responding to student emails and the average number of career publications. A small effect was observed for employment status regarding the average number of undergraduates receiving individual instruction and the number of committee memberships (see Table 2.7).

Supporting resources. The NSOPF asked respondents to rate various resources available to them as faculty members on the following scale: 1) poor, 2) fair, 3) good, 4) excellent, and 5) not available/not applicable/don't know. For the purpose of determining average ratings, all responses indicating not available/not applicable/don't know (5) were coded as missing. Variable means, *t*-tests, and Cohen's D statistics were used to explore faculty ratings of resource adequacy. Results indicate a significant difference between the ratings of full- and part-time faculty regarding most resources. Ratings of centralized computer facilities and studio/performance space were not significantly different

TABLE 2.6
USE OF TECHNOLOGY TO SUPPLEMENT INSTRUCTION BY
EMPLOYMENT STATUS

Demographics	Part-Time Row % (Column %)	Full-Time Row % (Column %)
Use Web Sites for Any Classes		
Yes	62.68 (34.06)	37.32 (35.04)
No	63.73 (65.94)	36.27 (64.91)
Use Email to Communicate With Students		
Yes	54.52 (34.05)	45.48 (49.12)
No	69.16 (65.95)	30.84 (50.88)
Percentage of Students Using Email to Communicate With Faculty		
Less than 20%	64.31 (90.14)	35.69 (86.55)
20%–39%	53.95 (2.66)	46.05 (3.93)
40%–59%	62.46 (3.76)	37.54 (3.91)
60%–79%	29.08 (0.32)	70.92 (1.35)
80% or more	55.87 (3.11)	44.13 (4.25)

Note: % represents weighted percentages.

among the two faculty groups. The remaining average ratings (e.g., laboratory space, Internet connections, classroom space, office space, etc.) were found to be significantly different according to employment status. With the exception of the availability of research assistants and office space, which were found to have a medium effect size, small effects were found for the remaining resources exhibiting a significant difference (see Table 2.8).

Faculty Attitudes and Opinions

Satisfaction. Faculty were asked to rate their level of satisfaction with respect to 15 items plus provide an overall rating of their job. Results

TABLE 2.7
FACULTY ACTIVITIES BY EMPLOYMENT STATUS

Faculty Activities	Part-Time	Full-Time
Average hours/week spent responding to student emails	2.9 hrs	2.8 hrs
** Average contact hours/week providing individual instruction to undergraduates	2.2 hrs	4.6 hrs
* Average number of undergraduates receiving individual instruction	7.3	13.6
*** Average total office hours/week	1.6 hrs	7.0 hrs
* Average number of committee memberships	0.3	0.6
Average number of career publications	6.8	7.6
*** Average hours/week on committee work	0.5 hrs	2.8 hrs
*** Average total hours worked/week	35.7 hrs	48.8 hrs

Note: Items marked with a single asterisk (*) are significant (alpha = 0.05) and exhibit a small effect. Double asterisks (**) indicate a significant medium effect, and triple asterisks (***) indicate a strong effect per Cohen (1988). Unmarked items are not significant at the 0.05 level.

indicate broad differences in satisfaction between full- and part-time faculty, with the exception of the authority to decide course content, the time available to advise students, and the availability of spousal employment opportunities. A significantly large effect was found between full- and part-time faculty satisfaction with benefits while medium effects were identified for differences in satisfaction for work load, job security, advancement opportunity, and freedom to do consulting (see Table 2.9).

Attitudes about the profession. Table 2.10 presents the study findings regarding the future employment intentions of full- and part-time faculty. Each possibility was found to be significant, with part-time

TABLE 2.8
RATINGS OF SUPPORTING RESOURCES BY FACULTY ACCORDING TO
EMPLOYMENT STATUS

Supporting Resources	Part-Time	Full-Time
* Research equipment/instruments	2.65	2.50
* Laboratory space and supplies	2.63	2.44
* Availability of teaching assistants	1.98	1.67
** Availability of research assistants	1.85	1.54
* Computers and local networks	2.84	3.00
Centralized computer facilities	2.89	2.86
* Internet connections	2.99	3.06
* Technical support for computers	2.83	2.67
* Audio/visual equipment	3.02	2.84
* Classroom space	2.93	2.74
** Office space	2.25	2.61
Studio/performance space	2.55	2.48
* Secretarial support	2.96	2.70
* Library holdings	2.77	2.57

Note: 1 = Poor; 2 = Fair; 3 = Good; 4 = Excellent.

Note: Items marked with a single asterisk (*) are significant (alpha = 0.05) and exhibit a small effect. Double asterisks (**) indicate a significant medium effect, and triple asterisks (***) indicate a strong effect per Cohen (1988). Unmarked items are not significant at the 0.05 level.

TABLE 2.9
FACULTY SATISFACTION BY EMPLOYMENT STATUS

Satisfaction With	Part-Time	Full-Time
Authority to decide course content	3.67	3.71
* Authority to decide courses taught	3.22	3.43
* Authority to make other job decisions	3.21	3.01
Time available to advise students	3.10	3.11
* Time available for class preparation	3.14	3.02
* Quality of undergraduate students	3.00	2.79
** Workload	3.28	2.95
** Job security	2.70	3.36
** Advancement opportunity	2.44	2.96
* Time to keep current in field	2.85	2.54
* Effectiveness of faculty leadership	2.85	2.61
** Freedom to do consulting	3.47	3.19
* Salary	2.54	2.70
*** Benefits	2.28	3.13
Spousal employment opportunities	3.09	3.16
* Overall job	3.23	3.32

Note: 1 = Very Dissatisfied; 2 = Somewhat Dissatisfied; 3 = Somewhat Satisfied; 4 = Very Satisfied.

Note: Items marked with a single asterisk (*) are significant (alpha = 0.05) and exhibit a small effect. Double asterisks (**) indicate a significant medium effect, and triple asterisks (***) indicate a strong effect per Cohen (1988). Unmarked items are not significant at the 0.05 level.

TABLE 2.10

FUTURE EMPLOYMENT INTENTIONS BY EMPLOYMENT STATUS

How likely is it that you will . . .	Part-Time	Full-Time
** Accept a part-time postsecondary job in 3 years	1.46	1.12
* Accept a full-time postsecondary job in 3 years	1.52	1.31
* Accept a part-time non-postsecondary job in 3 years	1.32	1.16
** Accept a full-time non-postsecondary job in 3 years	1.48	1.22
* Retire in three years	1.25	1.33

Note: 1 = Not at all likely; 2 = Somewhat likely; 3 = Very likely.

Note: Items marked with a single asterisk (*) are significant (alpha = 0.05) and exhibit a small effect. Double asterisks (**) indicate a significant medium effect, and triple asterisks (***) indicate a strong effect per Cohen (1988). Unmarked items are not significant at the 0.05 level.

faculty demonstrating a medium-sized increased likelihood of accepting a part-time postsecondary job in three years and accepting a full-time non-postsecondary job in three years, suggesting that part-time faculty are relatively mobile in their employment intentions compared with full-time faculty.

Our findings on the characteristics, attitudes, and opinions of full- and part-time faculty demonstrate the diversity in nature and purpose of this critical group. The following discussion of the implications of these trends provides guidance on the effective use of part-time faculty as the growth in this group continues to outpace the traditional cadre of full-time faculty.

Discussion

Today, higher education remains in great demand while economic resources are increasingly strained. The increased environment of accountability and emphasis on effectiveness and efficiency have resulted in many changes in institutions that are dependent on funding from public appropriations. In order to cope with stakeholder demand to do more with fewer resources, administrators have been forced to change the way institutions operate to better utilize the limited resources. Indeed, as Gellerman (1990) notes,

> the necessity for change is usually faced only when some kind of crisis arises: not because management failed to foresee the need, but because it bided its time until the most powerful opponents of change were forced to acknowledge that change was no longer avoidable. (p. 60)

Thus, as a labor-intensive enterprise, higher education has been forced to alter the manner in which faculty are employed to better utilize available resources. This study has shown that part-time faculty outnumber full-time faculty, signaling the reshaping of the faculty corps to better maximize limited resources.

Impact of Part-Time Faculty in American Higher Education

The changes that we see in the employment demographics of today's community college faculty will have an important impact on the structure and functioning of tomorrow's higher education system. In exploring the effects of this change in faculty employment, Baldwin and Chronister (2001) identify six consequences that institutions must consider when deciding to hire faculty in nontraditional (i.e., part-time) roles. First, part-time faculty provide a great deal of institutional flexibility. With short-term, contractual employees (typically hired for only one year, though sometimes on a semester basis), institutions have the option of non-renewing the contracts of temporary faculty for a variety of curricular or enrollment reasons; however, this action would be impossible with full-time, and in some two-year colleges, tenured faculty. Additionally, hiring short-term, contract faculty can facilitate experimentation with new academic programs or course offerings without the long-term commitment full-time faculty would necessitate. This option allows institutions to implement new offerings that quickly respond to changing market demands without committing the institution to those particular courses over the long term (Baldwin & Chronister, 2001). Because a major role of the community college is workforce development, a reliance on part-time faculty ensures the institution can deftly respond to emerging trends in the local economy. The hiring of part-time faculty also is of economic benefit to the institution because several part-time instructors can be hired in different specialties for the price of one full-time faculty member. Part-time instructors are usually paid much less per course than a regular faculty member and their part-time status typically means that the institution does not provide them with health and retirement benefits that would be due a full-time instructor (American Federation of Teachers, 2003).

Academically, the use of part-time faculty brings a mixed bag of advantages and concerns. Those hired for such positions are typically specialists in one area, which makes them attractive to the institutions. Usually, such faculty are exemplary teachers who have extensive experience in the private sector which they can draw on to engage students in the practical application of academic work. These faculty can bring a fresh perspective to the classroom, real-world experience that substantially augments the educational experience for students. However, at some institutions, part-time faculty teach heavy loads of large, introductory courses which can result in compromised quality and reduced student-faculty interaction. In addition, these part-time faculty may react to their insecure employment status by not bonding with the institution (Bach, 1999; Baldwin & Chronister, 2001). As a result, these faculty are constantly in the job market, which can create a revolving-door instructional environment for the institution.

The hiring of part-time faculty can also negatively impact relations with students. Often, part-time faculty are not required to serve as academic advisors, and with the growing numbers of students (whose numbers are being accommodated by the use of part-time faculty), the pressure for advising and mentoring on full-time faculty is dramatically growing. This demand on full-time faculty can lead to a loss of quality in the educational experience and problems with morale as full-time faculty can begin to feel overworked and part-time faculty may feel marginalized and possibly exploited (Baldwin & Chronister, 2001).

Initiatives for a Supportive Work Environment

As the results of this study indicate, part-time faculty will play a significant role in the future of public two-year institutions. Thus, it is imperative that institutions develop policies and practices that effectively integrate these faculty into the organizational culture and maximize their talents while providing a stimulating and meaningful work experience for the part-time or contract employee. As Bach (1999), Baldwin and Chronister (2001), and Breneman (1997) indicate, there are institutions today that have progressive policies in place which serve to compensate part-time faculty appropriately and integrate them into their institution's culture in a meaningful and rewarding way.

Initially, two-year colleges must hire part-time faculty in an open and ethical manner, with the full understanding by the candidates of the exact terms and expectations of the position. In an effort to ameliorate the employment security concerns and transient nature of part-time positions, Baldwin and Chronister (2001) and Breneman (1997) advocate for a fixed five-year term contract, with the institutional option of renewal upon satisfactory performance. It is critical that these performance standards are explicit and fairly applied to ensure an equitable review at the end of the contract term. In order to ease the perception of inferiority of part-time faculty, Baldwin and Chronister support the opportunity for meaningful involvement in faculty governance and curricular development. Finally, an equitable salary and benefits package are necessary to support the commitment and effort of part-time faculty (Bach, 1999; Baldwin & Chronister, 2001; Breneman, 1997). Essentially, the culture of American community colleges must change to reflect the circumstances of part-time faculty in such a manner as to validate the contributions of these faculty through an equitable system of work responsibilities, rewards, and compensation.

Directions for Further Research

While not examined in detail in this study, we anticipate that there are a variety of differences in activities and opinions of full- and part-time faculty according to their primary teaching field. This study demonstrated significant differences by broad discipline areas (occupational education and general education) and future research is needed to examine disciplinary subcultures in depth. For example, it is important to explore whether occupational programs that have programmatic accreditation (nursing, allied health, and engineering technologies) have a significantly greater percentage of full-time faculty when compared to faculty groups in mathematic and the humanities. In addition, research is needed on the impact of regional versus programmatic accreditation within different discipline areas and should explore the use and proliferation of part-time faculty in these disciplines to determine what the future holds if, as expected, the majority of faculty that teach general education are part-time, while those in occupational areas are predominantly full-time.

Another area for future research is the use of part-time faculty on student retention. The literature is replete with research that demonstrates that as faculty-student interaction increases, retention also increases (Endo & Harpel, 1982; Pascarella, 1980; Pascarella & Terenzini, 1977). The NSOPF-99 data demonstrate that part-time faculty spend less time outside of class advising students, have less access to email, and use email less to communicate with students than do full-time faculty. Additionally, part-time faculty have less access to office space, telephones, and the Internet. Students who select classes taught by part-time faculty may have less opportunity for student-faculty interaction outside the classroom than do students who select classes taught by full-time faculty.

Another area to examine is the impact of large numbers of part-time faculty on long-term institutional goals and programmatic quality. Generally, full-time faculty are the ones who comprise college committees and planning groups that develop the academic goals, frameworks, and processes that guide a college and its programmatic offerings. Part-time faculty are rarely involved in departmental or institutional policy or governance. For colleges with large percentages of part-time faculty it becomes the task of a small group of full-time faculty to do the work of the department, advising, curriculum development, program development, and institutional governance.

Summary and Conclusions

This chapter examined a variety of differences between a national sample of part-time and full-time community college faculty. The use of part-time faculty in community colleges continues to increase and the justification from administrators usually relates to financial issues. Our concern with this increase is one of academic integrity. This concern is not based on a lack of confidence in the preparation or teaching abilities of those part-timers, but rather on long-term institutional stability, student outcomes associated with large numbers of part-time faculty that have little input in instructional development, and departmental and institutional decision-making for the future of the college.

When conducting studies of faculty groups it is important to consider that on some characteristics the groups vary considerably and for others we see little difference. Knowing this context may be helpful as future researchers examine a variety of issues regarding the impact of faculty characteristics on the educational experience of students. This chapter provides a necessary orientation to part-time two-year college faculty within the context of their full-time peers and sets the stage for in-depth study of this vital group.

References

American Federation of Teachers. (2003, December 10). *The vanishing professor.* Washington, DC: Author. Retrieved July 26, 2004, from http://www.aft.org/pubs-reports/higher_ed/vanishing-professor.htm

Antony, J. S., & Valadez, J. R. (2002). Exploring the satisfaction of part-time college faculty in the Unites States. *Review of Higher Education, 26*(1), 41–56.

Bach, P. (1999, Spring). Part-time faculty are here to stay. *Planning for Higher Education, 27*(3), 32–40.

Baldwin, R. G., & Chronister, J. L. (2001). *Teaching without tenure: Policies and practices for a new era.* Baltimore, MD: Johns Hopkins University Press.

Breneman, D. W. (1997). *Alternatives to tenure for the next generation of academics* (New Pathways Working Paper Series, Inquiry #14). Washington, DC: American Association for Higher Education.

Cohen, J. (1988). *Statistical power analysis for the behavioral sciences* (2nd ed.). Mahwah, NJ: Lawrence Earlbaum.

Conley, V. M., Leslie, D. W., & Zimbler, L. J. (2002). Part-time instructional faculty and staff: Who they are, what they do, and what they think. *Education Statistics Quarterly, 4*(2), 97–103.

Endo, J. J., & Harpel, R. L. (1982). The effects of student-faculty interaction on students' educational outcomes. *Research in Higher Education, 16*(2), 115–136.

Erwin, J., & Andrews, H. A. (1993). State of part-time faculty services at community colleges in a nineteen state region. *Community College Journal of Research and Practice, 17*(6), 555–562.

Gellerman, S. W. (1990). In organizations, as in architecture, form follows function. *Organizational Dynamics, 19*(3), 57–68.

Keim, M. C. (1989). Two-year college faculty: A research update. *Community College Review, 17*(3), 34–43.

Leslie, D. W., & Gappa, J. M. (2002). Part-time faculty: Competent and committed. In C. L. Outcalt (Ed.), *New directions for community colleges: No. 118. Community college faculty: Characteristics, practices, and challenges* (pp. 59–67). San Francisco, CA: Jossey-Bass.

Liu, M., Finkelstein, M. J., & Schuster, J. H. (2002, October). *Understanding the other half: Change and continuity in the part-time professoriate.* Paper presented at the 2002 ASHE Conference, Portland, OR.

Pascarella, E. T. (1980). Student-faculty informal contact and college outcomes. *Review of Educational Research, 50*(4), 545–595.

Pascarella, E. T., & Terenzini, P. T. (1977). Patterns of student-faculty informal interaction beyond the classroom and voluntary freshman attrition. *Journal of Higher Education, 68*(5), 540–552.

Pollack, J. S. (1986, January/February). The erosion of tenure in the California State University. *Academe,* 19–24.

Pratt, L. R. (1997). Disposable faculty: Part-time exploitation as management strategy. In C. Nelson (Ed.), *Will teach for food: Academic labor in crisis* (pp. 264–277). Minneapolis, MN: University of Minnesota Press.

Roueche, J. E., Roueche, S. D., & Milliron, M. D. (1996). In the company of strangers: Addressing the utilization and integration of part-time faculty in American community colleges. *Community College Journal of Research and Practice, 20*(2), 105–117.

Schuetz, P. (2002). Instructional practices of part-time and full-time faculty. In C. L. Outcalt (Ed.), *New directions for community colleges: No. 118. Community college faculty: Characteristics, practices, and challenges* (pp. 39–46). San Francisco, CA: Jossey-Bass.

Thomas, S. L., & Heck, R. H. (2001). Analysis of large-scale secondary data in higher education research: Potential perils associated with complex sample designs. *Research in Higher Education, 42*(5), 517–540.

Truell, A. D., Price, W. T., & Joyner, R. L. (1998). Satisfaction among community college occupational technical faculty. *Community College Journal of Research and Practice, 22*(2), 111–122.

U.S. Department of Education, National Center for Education Statistics. (1997). *Instructional faculty and staff in higher education institutions: Fall 1987 and fall 1992.* Washington, DC: Author.

U.S. Department of Education, National Center for Education Statistics. (2002). *1999 national study of postsecondary faculty (NSOPF:99): Methodology Report.* Washington, DC: Author.

3 | Adjunct Faculty as Valued Members of the Academy

Eduardo J. Marti

The community college sector operates in an open admissions environment and longs for the agony and the ecstasy enjoyed by the four-year colleges of filling their fall class in May and having all summer to prepare for the arrival of a carefully selected group of first-time students. In the "retail" environment of open admissions, community colleges open their doors in September not knowing the size of their entering class until after classes have started. Therefore, flexibility is the key to the survival of a community college, and the adjunct corps of faculty members is extremely important in managing this chaotic environment. Community colleges need to be able to call up the "adjunct reserves" when the student enrollment soars and to diminish the instructional ranks with ease when the enrollment wanes. A strong corps of adjunct faculty members is essential for community colleges. In this chapter, the benefits and drawbacks of having a corps of adjunct faculty members and the issue of quality of instruction will be explored. The chapter will conclude with a set of recommendations.

The National Picture

According to the National Center for Education Statistics (NCES), 43% of post-secondary instructional faculty members work part-time (U.S. Department of Education, 2002).

The percentage of part-time faculty varies by type of school: 66% at community colleges, 41% at four-year private schools, and 27% at public four-year colleges. . . . The lower percentage of part-time faculty at 4-year institutions does not necessarily translate to more teaching by full-time faculty. In 1993, in addition to 184,000 part-time faculty positions, there were some 200,000 graduate assistants in 4-year institutions with graduate programs. (Miller, 2001, The Numbers Section, ¶ 3)

A carefully recruited pool of potential adjunct faculty members is an asset to any college. As of October 2002, 27% of adjuncts held advanced degrees as reported by NCES (U.S. Department of Education, 2002). There are many authors, engineers, businesspeople, and craftspeople that, as successful professionals, see teaching as the culmination of their achievements. They teach while practicing their profession. Adjunct employment enables them to come in contact with eager minds and allows them to share the fruits of their accumulated labors. They bring real-world experience to the classroom and they can serve as good contacts for the future employment of students.

Optimum Size of the Adjunct Faculty Corps

There is a continuing debate as to what should be the optimum percentage of instruction delivered by adjunct faculty members. Those who advocate for a high full-time/part-time ratio claim that there are dangers in an over-reliance on adjuncts to deliver our instruction. Adjunct faculty members are truly "contracted professionals" who, in most cases, are not part of the complete academic enterprise. Their connection to the college is likely to end when the class ends. It is rare to find an adjunct professor involved in the governance of the college or attending college-wide committee meetings. In general, the extracurricular activities where one can find members of the adjunct corps are in departmental meetings and in those activities that appeal to them as professionals, for example, professional development, athletic events, and some student activities. While they may be excellent instructors, they are not full members of the college.

Others say that there is no difference in the quality of instruction if appropriate training is provided and if there are sufficient support services in the institution. If one subscribes to a model that relies on a strong administration, depends less on the collegial model, and sees faculty members simply as deliverers of instruction, then it stands to reason that excellence in the classroom is sufficient. These proponents point to the lack of significant difference in retention rates in those schools that use a large percentage of adjunct faculty members as compared to those with more full-time faculty members (Roueche, Roueche, & Milliron, 1995). Another factor that comes into play is the maturity of the institution. If a college has well-established standard operating procedures, with a clear division of responsibilities, sufficient support services to provide necessary advising, mentoring, and guidance, a governance plan that does not require significant participation by all the members of the college community, then it is reasonable to expect that the percentage of instruction delivered by part-time faculty would have no effect on the quality of the educational services provided to the students.

Whether one subscribes to one school of thought or the other, the fact remains that for the student in the classroom, the person delivering the lecture or managing the learning activity is "The Professor." As far as the student is concerned, there is no difference between the full-time, seasoned professor and the businesswoman who is fully engaged in her profession but who teaches one evening class per week. Of course, there are many variants of this continuum. The task of a good academic administrator is to manage each faculty member individually and to ensure that the standards of the college are maintained.

The Importance of Clear Expectations

The hiring process for adjuncts is different from that utilized to select a full-time faculty member. Generally, to fill a full-time faculty opening there is a national search, a college or departmental screening committee, a background check and, in some cases, a sample lecture is required. The process can take anywhere from three to six months. Rarely is someone hired on a full-time basis without a solid teaching record and publications or a demonstrated potential to achieve in the academic environment. On the other hand, to fill a part-time faculty opening, the department generally searches locally, there may or may not be a departmental screening committee, and in-depth background checks are unusual. Rarely is there an opportunity to see the applicant deliver a lecture or conduct a class, and the requirements for advanced degrees or demonstrated experience in the academy are less stringent. Often, academic administrators are desperately trying to fill a class and they rely on the fact that this is a nontenure-track appointment and that there is the flexibility not to rehire the following semester.

Since the hiring process for an adjunct instructor can be less rigorous than that for a full-time faculty member, it is very important to have a clear set of departmental expectations for the newly appointed part-time member of the faculty. Most colleges have a part-time faculty handbook that provides pertinent information to the new faculty members. Most handbooks contain chapters discussing excused absences, paid substitutions, classroom observations, college email accounts and policies, final grade and attendance rosters, adjunct benefits, the semester calendar, and more.

Most colleges also have a general orientation session for new adjunct faculty members. These "talking heads" sessions serve the purpose of providing an overview to the new arrivals of how the college functions and an opportunity for the administration to delineate current initiatives and to give the new part-time faculty a sense that they are an important component of the college community. The training offered at a local fast food store often is more intensive than that provided to a newly hired adjunct faculty member. Yet the expectations on the part of the student of the adjunct and the student of the full-time faculty member are equal.

The role of the department chair is crucial in maintaining high standards of quality among the instructional corps. As adjunct faculty members generally are not professional teachers, and as most of the new adjunct faculty members have little or no formal training in pedagogy, it is imperative that a program of on-the-job-training be carefully delineated. It is important that there be a series of meetings, throughout the semester, between the adjunct faculty members and the chair or the chair's designee. The person must be given a general orientation on classroom comportment, students' rights, grading methodology, techniques to manage disruptive students, sexual harassment and departmental policies, as well as many other topics. This cannot be addressed in a one- hour meeting. Also, adjunct faculty members should be urged to attend faculty development workshops. These workshops should address different modalities of instruction and help the adjunct faculty members learn about teaching techniques. Some colleges have incentives for adjuncts to attend these workshops. In some cases, there is additional compensation associated with the completion of a certain number of hours of training. While in most cases the training is voluntary, there is a good case to be made for making training a requirement.

The Evaluation

Most colleges have an evaluation process for adjunct faculty members. There is usually a classroom observation and student evaluations. Classroom observations are conducted by senior members of the department. The adjunct faculty member may or may not be informed of the date and time of the visit depending on institutional culture or a collective bargaining contract. During the visit, the students know that something is different in this particular session. Sometimes, it is very clear that there is an evaluator in the room, other times the evaluator is so unobtrusive that the audience quickly forgets the foreign presence in the classroom. Most evaluators come into the activity disposed to give the adjunct instructor a positive evaluation. The reports generally address very simple elements such as clarity of objectives of the lesson, the instructor's demeanor, classroom management, and student interaction. It is at best cursory, and it must be seen as only one of the tools necessary to judge the efficacy of the adjunct instructor.

Experienced evaluators know what constitutes good teaching in their respective disciplines and, for the most part, are successful at spotting the good instructors. Recognizing the weaknesses is more difficult. As teachers, the need to nurture creates the natural tendency to praise the effort and point out the areas of strength. Evaluators should be aware that their function is to protect the integrity of the department and if they see any cause of concern, the appropriate action is to notify the department chair. The role of the department chair is to coach the adjunct faculty members and, very specifically, to point out the areas needing improvement and provide sufficient documentation. This is especially true in colleges where the adjunct faculty members are part of a collective bargaining unit. Student observations are another method of evaluation. However, as students may be afraid of retaliation, senior administrators or departmental committees often do not hear about problems with a particular instructor until after the semester has ended. Even after the semester ends, it has to be a fairly serious situation for the students to complain. Student evaluations that contain narratives are more helpful than those that provide a numerical average of the responses.

In reality, the decision to rehire the adjunct faculty member is a subjective one. All the objective measures are but tools that assist the department chair and others charged with making the decision.

The Unionized Environment

Associations, unions, or any other recognized collective bargaining unit is necessary only when there is a consistent lack of communication among the different constituencies of the college. After all, a union is akin to hiring a lawyer. One only resorts to this expensive method of defense when one feels threatened or when normal communications break down. However, unions are not necessarily the enemy. While the relationship between union and management is by definition adversarial, if there is mutual respect, standards of behavior can be established that benefit all involved.

Unions attempt to ensure that the collective bargaining agreement is applied evenly and appropriately. Sometimes this is interpreted as a celebration of mediocrity, especially by administrators who are not familiar with the nuances of the contract. The need to have adequate documentation before taking a personnel action is sometimes seen as an interference with good management. It increases the need for bureaucracy and is seen as unnecessary and far removed from the real work of the academy. Unionization may be counterintuitive to the collegial approach that is the foundation of the academy, but in many areas, the union has become a necessity because of perceived excesses by administrators and/or trustees, because of local culture, or because of external influences.

Academic administrators must be familiar with the contract and its application to part-time faculty. The contract is a limitation of management's prerogatives. It is not an enabling document; it places restrictions on management. It is collectively bargained and the agreement codifies the behavior but from the point of view of setting limits. The middle managers, the people who have the responsibility of administering the agreement, must be well versed with the nuances of the contract.

As most personnel decisions are made at the departmental level, it is difficult to ensure equity and quality across the college or university unless the department chair or the dean takes the time to really understand the contract. One useful practice is to use common documentation of the actions leading to personnel decisions. Having the labor relations designee meet with the academic department chairs on a periodic basis to discuss the administration of the contract, and finding a common language to describe deficiencies and accomplishments is helpful. Sharing best practices in coaching adjunct faculty members is always useful and it is a good investment of time.

Training evaluators is essential for a well-run department in a unionized environment. It is important for the department to come to terms as to the particular departmental criteria within the umbrella of the college or university criteria and that which is permissible under the restrictions imposed by the union contract. Once the criteria are established, the department must come together and agree on a set of expected behaviors that are consonant with the established criteria. The codification of these agreements is highly desirable to establish a departmental culture of mutual trust and respect, to minimize the possibility of having an individual or a group of individuals rule by the power of their personality rather than by application of a well-established and well-codified set of behaviors resulting from their collective wisdom.

As teachers, it is difficult to commit to paper all the areas that need improvement, including student evaluations, in an adjunct faculty member's performance. When areas needing attention are found, there is a tendency to be gentle. As many adjunct faculty members come from a different and harsher environment, an environment where criticism is given with greater directness, the gentle approach of the academy sometimes is misinterpreted. The expectations that will guide the evaluation process must be very clear, and this will help the adjunct faculty members to understand the colleges's academic mores well.

Value of the Adjunct Faculty Member to the Institution

Academic homeostasis depends on a well-balanced combination of the deliberateness of wisdom that comes with an experienced department and the brash enthusiasm and propensity for risk-taking that is brought by a less experienced group of scholars. A department is, after all, a microcosm of the college. It should have a mission, goals, and objectives which are consonant with the college. It should have clearly articulated expectations of its members, based on the traditions forged over time. It should welcome change that is evolutionary and that augments, rather than supplants, the traditions of the department. The adjunct faculty members's corps can be very useful to the department. Their freshness of thought can be exciting and stimulating for the continued evolution of the departmental vision. This energy can only be harnessed if the newcomer is welcomed and trusted.

Carefully selected adjunct faculty members can bring to the department a wealth of experiences. A lawyer discussing a legal principle using an actual case, a nurse discussing a disease using a personal encounter with a patient suffering from it, a real estate agent discussing a difficult closing while demonstrating the need for appropriate research of a title, all bring with them the immediacy of reality that enriches the classroom.

Transition From Part-Time to Full-Time

Many part-time faculty members make the transition from adjunct to full-time members of a department. This is especially true for the recent Ph.D. who starts teaching as an adjunct because there is no full-time position available. But it also could be a retiring professional who begins teaching on a part-time basis while transitioning from the practice to retirement.

It is easy to understand why departments tend to favor adjunct faculty members who apply for a full-time position. The individual has a proven track record in the department, with the students, with the institution. The individual has established friendships among the department's faculty and is familiar with the institution. A part-time faculty member who accepts a full-time appointment requires less orientation and thus can free scarce human resources to attend to other pressing matters.

However, hiring full-time faculty solely from the adjunct ranks can lead to lack of progress in affirmative action efforts if the part-time pool is not sufficiently diverse. As searches for full-time faculty members are advertised in professional journals and publications with a national audience, the chances of obtaining a more diverse applicant pool are greatly enhanced. The conversion of an adjunct to a full-time faculty member is a good option to consider but must be balanced by other institutional and departmental goals.

Summary and Conclusions

- **Determine the optimum part-time to full-time ratio for the institution.** As the allocation of available lines is made, it is important for academic administrators to look at the overall distribution of the instructional membership. This must be done institution-wide as well as department by department. Similarly, the ethnic composition of each department should be assessed and compared to the available workforce data. This will provide each department with a set of expectations as they go through the hiring process.
- **Determine to what extent the adjunct corps is important to the governance of the college.** The faculty governance structure determines the policy that, upon the recommendation of the president and the acceptance by the board of trustees, becomes the rules of behavior for the institution. Therefore, it is important that, at the departmental level, the adjunct faculty members be well-informed.
- **Hire well; fire fast.** Hiring adjunct faculty members is an important activity of the department chair and/or designee. If there is any question as to the competency of an adjunct faculty member, the appropriate action is to document, coach deficiencies, and if there is no significant improvement, nonrenewal.

- **Do not give cause to the adjuncts to organize.** If there is no collective bargaining representing adjunct faculty, pay careful attention to personnel practices and support for this cohort.
- **Establish procedures to convert adjuncts to full-timers while preserving the tenets of affirmative action.**
- **Protect the integrity of the academic department.** While it is desirable for a president to be proactive in recruiting as many adjunct faculty as possible, it is important that the recruiting overtures be made in general terms. The department, through a peer process, selects the candidates that ultimately become adjunct faculty.

Clearly, adjunct faculty members are an important component of American community colleges. Community colleges depend on adjunct faculty members to help them adjust to the flexible requirements of admissions patterns, to bring expertise to the classroom that otherwise would not be available for students, and to invigorate the curriculum. Adjuncts can be a great asset to colleges. If managed and supported sufficiently and sensitively, they will become valued members of the academy.

References

Miller, R. (2001, September). *Use of part-time faculty in higher education: Numbers and impact.* Washington, DC: American Association of Colleges and Universities. Retrieved June 7, 2004, from http://www. greaterexpectations.org/briefing_papers/parttimefaculty.html

Roueche, J. E., Roueche, S. D., & Milliron, M. D. (1995). *Strangers in their own land: Part-time faculty in American community colleges.* Washington, DC: Community College Press.

U.S. Department of Education, National Center for Education Statistics. (2002). *A profile of part-time faculty: Fall 1998.* Washington, DC: Author. Retrieved July 26, 2004, from http://nces.ed.gov/pubs2002/200208.pdf

4 | ENCULTURATION AND DEVELOPMENT OF PART-TIME FACULTY

Kristel D. Phillips and Dale F. Campbell

Part-time faculty are growing in number among all community colleges. As of 1995, 75% of faculty at public community colleges were part-time (Leslie & Gappa, 2002). This growth has brought forward concerns regarding credentials, experience, and levels of effectiveness of the part-time faculty member. Typically, however, student evaluations and exit exams have shown no difference in the quality of instruction between full- and part-time instructors (Leslie & Gappa, 2002; Miller, Finley, & Vancko, 2000).

Accepting that quality of instruction by part-timers is comparable to quality of instruction by full-timers, community colleges need to focus on integrating the part-time instructor more fully into the institution through professional development and evaluation so that the students will fully benefit from their expertise (Commission on the Future of Community Colleges, 1988). Statistically, part-time faculty are the least likely to receive invitations to this type of institutional training and support, though they make up a majority of the faculty (Roueche, Roueche, & Milliron, 1995).

As found in one study, part-time faculty were satisfied with being part-time, but stated they do not participate as active members within their departments, or even interact much professionally, unless they need help with something (Wien, 2002). Burnstad (2003) further suggests,

To implement a comprehensive program for the inclusion of part-time faculty, an institution should have the following: A climate and culture of inclusion; a recognition of the value of part-time faculty as integral to the success of the college in meeting student needs; institutional leadership and vision; and support systems . . . (p. 24)

Quite often, however, faculty development programs overlook the basics and offer programs that include only full-time instructors, are of short duration, cover several topics in a year, and have little application or time to reflect. It is for these reasons that many faculty development programs produce little or no improvement in teaching and, therefore, learning (Katz & Henry, 1988). Including part-time faculty in good faculty development programs could only serve to enhance the quality of instruction and the mission of the institution.

Faculty Development in Florida Community Colleges

The purpose of this chapter is to discuss the results of a status report on faculty development in Florida community colleges, with particular focus on development of part-time faculty. The research is a modified replication of the work done by Caffey (1978). Full- and part-time mathematics and communications instructors were asked their opinions on what goals they felt the institution held as important, what goals and activities they thought were important, and what programs they perceived were available to them. Results were analyzed overall, by full- and part-time status, by discipline, and by institution where appropriate.

The vice presidents of instruction at each of the 28 colleges were contacted by mail and email and invited to participate. Twenty-one colleges chose to participate in the study. Participating vice presidents were then sent an email memo detailing the location of the survey web site that could be forwarded to their faculty, and/or were sent paper copies of the survey that could be placed in faculty mailboxes as needed. Both versions contained a memo from the vice president that could be forwarded to the faculty indicating their support of the survey. Each college then had one month to complete the survey, and weekly reminders were sent by email.

Results

Two-hundred and eighty-seven surveys out of 1,196 were received (24%). This return rate is slightly higher than others who have tried to include a significant number of part-time faculty (Gerity, 1999; Roark, 1989). After removing 32 surveys that did not meet the qualifications of this study, it was found that of those that participated (257 total), 55% of the respondents were full-time faculty, compared to 45% part-time faculty; 63% were mathematics faculty, while 37% were communications faculty. Within those groups, 53% were full-time and 47% were part-time mathematics faculty; with 59% full-time and 41% part-time communications faculty reporting. The age range in this study went from 21–79 years, with the modal age being 51 years and the average age being 47.80.

Perception of Goals

More than 50% of the full-time faculty agreed that their institutions held the following goals (listed in order of preference) as important:

1) Enhancing/expanding classroom teaching and learning techniques (online instruction, collaborative learning, using case studies, small groups, etc.)
2) Facilitating the faculty's effective use of available instructional resources, technology, and services
3) Helping faculty to understand their own institution's mission and goals
4) Helping faculty adapt their teaching to changing social and economic conditions in the community and the world
5) Providing an understanding of the institution's policies, procedures, and decision-making processes
6) Increasing faculty's knowledge of the characteristics of their students and helping them use that knowledge to provide better instruction
7) Keeping faculty informed about administrative decisions affecting them and their work

8) Familiarizing faculty with the distinctive role of the community college
9) Enhancing the faculty's knowledge in their subject areas

Overall, more than 50% of the part-time faculty agreed with the full-time faculty that their institutions held the same goals as important, the exceptions the exclusion of goal number six and the inclusion of the goal "Familiarizing faculty with the distinctive role of the community college." Interestingly, all of the goals listed by the faculty were consistently rated as institutional goals by less of the part-time faculty.

It is noteworthy that less than 55% of all faculty thought that the following were goals of the institution:

1) Enhancing the faculty's knowledge in their subject areas
2) Creating harmonious working relationships among departments and divisions
3) Improving human relationship skills
4) Helping faculty cope with personal needs

Importance of Goals and Activities

In answering the question, "What types of professional development activities and institutional goals are perceived to be important to full-time and part-time mathematics and communications instructors at their institutions?" little difference was found.

Overall in terms of goals, both full- and part-time faculty were concerned with improving classroom instruction via improved knowledge and capabilities regarding students, and teaching and learning techniques. While administrative decisions were considered important, understanding the role of the community college and its policies and processes were not.

These results agree with Caffey's (1978) original research in this area, where he also found "Improvement of teaching skills, enhancing the instructor's knowledge in the subject area, and motivating faculty members to strive for excellence in their performance as teachers" were listed as primary goals of importance. Fourth listed was tied between "Faculty knowledge of student characteristics" and "Inform faculty of administrative decisions." "Effective use of instructional resources," and "Adapt teaching to changing conditions" rounded out the top seven. His participating full-time faculty also tended to devalue goals relating to institutional mission, role, policies, and procedures.

That faculty were not concerned with the unique role of the community college should be of concern to both groups and their administrators. As the community changes, and the college changes to meet the needs of that community, faculty must have a clear understanding of what the institution is doing, and why they are doing it in that particular manner in order to teach the diverse student population they are facing.

Activities most valued by all full-time faculty were:

1) Orientation programs for faculty new to the school
2) Travel money to attend professional meetings
3) On-campus workshops on topics of professional interest to faculty
4) Financial support for advanced graduate study and/or research activities

In the current study, the three activities most disliked by all full-time faculty were:

1) Retreats
2) Videotaping and reviewing practice teaching sessions with faculty colleagues
3) Consultant visits to campus

In the original Caffey (1978) study, there were 10 items that received unfavorable rating from as many as 20% of the participants. Four items involved evaluation or observation, two involved activities to encourage faculty interaction, and two others involved assisting faculty with personal needs. It would *appear* that time and/or education has significantly altered the perception of what is desirable; however, two of the three items found in this study fall into two of those same categories: Retreats fall into encouraging faculty interaction and videotaping and review would fall into Caffey's evaluation and observation.

Activities most valued by all part-time faculty were:

1) Orientation programs for faculty new to the school
2) Access to professional development materials in the campus library
3) Graduate courses for credit, offered on campus, or at a nearby university

Items part-time faculty disliked were identical to the full-time faculty:

1) Videotaping and review of practice teaching sessions with faculty colleagues
2) Consultant visits to campus
3) Retreats

Availability

In answering the question, "Are these activities available to you?" many more full-time faculty perceived availability than did the part-time faculty. For example, 11 activities were seen as available by more than 50% of the responding full-time faculty, whereas only four activities were seen as available by more than 50% of the responding part-time faculty. Institutions varied as to the number of activities available, and between disciplines there were often discrepancies *within* the full- or part-time rankings as to whether activities were available or not.

Analysis

When the mathematics and communications faculty in the Florida Community Colleges were surveyed, it was discovered that the full- and part-time faculty are very similar in terms of what they perceive as goals of their institutions and what they perceive as important in terms of professional development activities. However, the part-time faculty appear to not have the same information available to them to make certain decisions, like whether particular goals are in fact goals within their institution. Also, they either do not have the information concerning the available activities, or they do not have access to the same professional development activities as the full-time faculty, as their perception of availability of activities was significantly different than the full-time faculty.

It seems imperative to include both full-time and adjunct faculty in the professional development programs that are offered (Sparks, 1983). It is often a fact that many instructors (full- or part-time), who participate in well-designed professional development programs walk away with many new ideas about how to improve their teaching, as well as more vital information concerning the institution and its practices and goals.

In a study done at 14 institutions involving over 900 faculty, 61% stated that they had introduced a new technique or approach in their teaching as a result of being involved in the faculty development program. Of these, 89% stated that it had improved their teaching effectiveness in some way. A final important point is that not only did the faculty feel their skills were enhanced but they also felt they had a greater appreciation for their institution, institutional practices, better relationships with more faculty at their institution, and a greater understanding of the administration and their students. Thus, they were less insulated from other departments within the institution and more aware of their students (Gaff & Morstain, 1978).

However, while it seems obvious that part-time faculty should be included in the development programming, a much more common outcome is that reported in research done by Grant (2000). In a study of 230 community colleges nationwide, it was found that 90% of the institutions had a formal faculty development program, and all had some form of development for their adjuncts. However, *none* of the colleges had programs designed especially for the needs of adjunct instructors, with the exception of a faculty handbook at a few of the institutions.

In a study completed in 1982, Leslie, Kellans, and Gunne reported that 84% of the colleges and universities provided no formal orientation for part-time faculty, and less than half of those surveyed stated they made syllabi available for the new part-timers. Finally, it was reported that only 31% of the community colleges surveyed provided a formal orientation (Leslie et al., 1982). In a separate study completed on the Washington community colleges, it was found that as the ratio of full-time to part-time faculty *decreased,* the number of personal development activities such as stress management, time management, and interpersonal skill development increased (Anderson, 1990).

Barriers to Involving Part-Time Faculty

Cost is the primary issue. However, the cost for funding a program for adjuncts seems even more expensive when it is realized that some that are trained today might not be at the college in three months. Justification of these expenses is difficult at best, especially if one has a board or an administration that does not understand the adjunct's value to the college (Miller et al., 2000; Richardson, 1992). Roueche et al. (1995) argued, on the other hand, that adjuncts were not really much less expensive if the institution was involving them the way they should in terms of enculturation and development.

Another barrier is logistics. Adjuncts typically have jobs other than at the college, so scheduling events, classes, and even orientations is very frustrating for everyone involved (Richardson, 1992). Given the varied schedules, more than one of the same event might have to be scheduled. As a result full-time faculty will have to accommodate the adjuncts' schedules in order to meet with them and to mentor them (Maguire, 1983; Richardson, 1992).

A third issue is politics. Adjuncts are hired out of convenience to the college based on enrollment and available finances. They are often considered at best of minimal importance to the institution and at worst dispensable (Cox, 2000; Gappa & Leslie, 1993; Roueche et al., 1995). Therefore, if a college chooses to invest in adjuncts either financially or through development programs or both, in some cases, they have been perceived as promoting "hopeful" future employment or tenure. (Although, if an institution had clear policies and intentions, this became a non-issue [Bach, 1999; Board of Regents of State College v. Roth, 1972; Perry v. Sinderman, 1972].)

Full-time faculty have expressed concern that the extensive use of part-time faculty is unfair and an assault on the tenure process (Naparsteck, 1991). With the lower pay, incentives, and attention that adjuncts receive, adjuncts are unionizing throughout the country in order to be recognized and treated more fairly (Leatherman, 2000a, 2000b, 2001; Naparsteck, 1991; Smallwood, 2003). Some authors questioned whether this morale issue would have materialized if the adjuncts had been drawn into the various aspects of the college through caring full-time faculty, staff, and administrators, and had been given the opportunity to further enhance their skills and knowledge (Maguire, 1983; Wyles, 1998).

> There are often psychological factors which inhibit this kind of collegiality. The adjunct may feel exploited, isolated, and diminished, with minimal status despite the importance and value of his contribution. Moreover, the college may not be too forthcoming to the adjunct in terms of information, support services, or just simple, professional courtesy, making an already difficult situation worse. When an instructor is paid only for his/her physical presence in the classroom, it defines an instructor in the worse way possible. It negates professional growth, class preparation . . . and defines them as worthless. (Maguire, 1983, p. 31)

There are several other identified barriers to providing programs for part-time instructors. A large one, which needs to be readily addressed, is lack of communication between administrators and part-time faculty concerning what the part-time faculty member needs to succeed. Several examples can be found in the literature to demonstrate that what each group deems important to the part-time faculty member's growth, the other deems less or unimportant (Byrd, 1986; Klenk, 1996; Rhodes, 1991; Roark, 1989; Tuck, 1981).

Other studies (Denman, 1986; Piasta, 1991; Roark, 1989) found that administrators and part-time faculty perceived needs very differently, and as a result, the institutions were not meeting the needs of their part-time faculty. These discrepancies, it seems, could be recognized earlier simply by surveying the persons involved before the program was designed (Moe, 1977).

Another barrier that could be addressed by institutions is ensuring that adjunct instructors have accurate information concerning what development programs are available to them throughout the year. In a study done by Byrd (1986), staff development officers and part-time instructors at three community colleges in Florida were surveyed comparing what the officers said was available in terms of faculty development opportunities and what the adjuncts thought was available. The results were that over 75% of the adjuncts at Broward Community College, over 50% at Florida Community College at Jacksonville, and over 90% at St. Johns River Community College were not aware of the training areas available to them. Furthermore, some adjunct faculty believed that certain training was available, when in fact it was not.

It is imperative that institutions include their part-time faculty in basic communications as much as possible. While many institutions require email addresses of all of their students, those same institutions may not have email addresses for 50%–60% of their faculty. The part-time faculty are valuable assets to the institution, just as full-time faculty or students are, and must be treated as such. Depending on word-of-mouth or even paper memos is not an effective means to communicate in what is quickly becoming a paperless society where situations and outcomes change literally overnight, especially in education. Communication with all faculty is vital to keeping an institution current and learning centered.

At times, the aforementioned issues and barriers make it difficult for institutions to be convinced that part-time faculty development is worthwhile. However, since part-time faculty comprise an average of 66% of the instructional workforce, teach more than 40% of the credit courses (especially the introductory undergraduate courses), and teach over one-fourth of all college classes offered, it has been suggested that community colleges find a way that is economically and legally satisfying to assist their adjuncts in fulfilling the institutional mission of improving learning (American Association of Community Colleges, 1997; Bach, 1999; Cox 2000; Roueche et al., 1995). In addition, it is felt that students, and therefore the institution, would benefit greatly from the expertise of adjuncts, who were generally practitioners in their fields and had the potential to open doors for both students and the college as a result of their community connections (Lyons, 1996). Furthermore, if the institution's mission is ultimately to produce learning (Barr & Tagg, 1995; Tinto, 1998), then a way is needed to draw adjuncts into the culture of the institution and the departments so as to best serve the students (Burnstad, 2003; Lyons, 1996).

Adjunct Participation in Professional Development

Part-time faculty are often perceived as uninterested, too busy, or unconcerned with participating in faculty development programs. Byrd's (1986) study showed little interest in participating overall; however, there was a tendency for part-time faculty to participate in selected areas when they were aware of availability. At both of the community colleges surveyed, the staff development officers reported a low level of awareness and participation by the adjunct instructors.

Illustrating the opposite, Roark (1989) asked adjuncts at three community colleges what formats of in-service activities they preferred. Out of the 15 formats offered, the adjuncts were allowed to check as many as they desired. Two-thirds of the adjuncts expressed interest in tuition-free courses, and over half expressed interest in attending departmental meetings. One-third were interested in attending college social events and/or seminars and/or general faculty meetings. Almost half cited attending half-day seminars, fall and spring planning sessions, new part-time faculty orientation sessions, and/or attending two-hour sessions one evening a week for a set number of weeks. Roark also found that 45% stated they would participate in a development program if offered at a convenient time, even if they were not paid. Another 50% stated they would participate if they were paid the same as they received for teaching, with only 4% stating that they would not participate. When asked when they would prefer to see development opportunities offered, over half of Roark's participants stated they would participate if the programs were offered right before a term began. The others were split fairly evenly between stating that the development program should begin within the first couple of weeks of the term or during the summer. If offered right before or soon after classes began, about 95% of the participants said they would attend.

Tuck (1981) found that 51% of those surveyed would participate if the program were offered at a convenient time. Another 34% stated they would participate if compensated in some form. Only 5.1% stated they would not participate.

One answer to participation by adjuncts (and full-time faculty, for that matter) may be to adapt the flexible calendar program that was instituted by the California Community College System. This program permitted the districts to designate up to 15 teaching days as paid non-teaching days for the expressed purpose of development activities (Alfano, 1993). Since extra, out-of-class time would not be required to attend the development sessions, it would be easier to draw in the intended populations.

Model Programs

While there were many institutions that provided a handbook or an orientation, there were few colleges that provided much more for adjunct instructors regardless of the size of the institution. For example, as of the 2000 spring semester, Johnson County Community College (JCCC), with approximately 68% adjunct faculty and over 16,000 credit students, provided adjuncts with paid sick leave, pay grades, and title tied to professional development activities and tuition reimbursement for credit classes. The college also required yearly orientation for all adjuncts, where the adjuncts received packets of ideas and teaching tips and a check-off sheet for needed items for the semester to help keep organized (Burnstad, 2000). Furthermore, by the spring of 2002, JCCC reported providing the following support and amenities for their part-time faculty: sample syllabi for courses; office space in addition to a private conferencing area; business cards and notepads; identical annual percentage increases in salary as all other college employees; pay for attending orientation, department meetings, committee work, and other required duties; mentors; evaluation procedures similar to full-time faculty; representatives on the adjunct advisory council; opportunity for financial support for various types of professional development; and recognition for years of service to the college (Burnstad, 2003).

Jackson Community College, a school in with 8,000 students, provided adjuncts with an orientation, and adjuncts were invited to attend college planning board meetings, department meetings, and college-wide social events. The college also provided an evening administrator specifically for adjunct faculty whom they could contact with questions and concerns. Adjuncts received an incentive of $30.00 stipend for each one-half day event they attended. The college often employed new adjuncts a semester ahead and paid them a stipend to sit through classes and/or labs that they would be teaching the following term. The institution provided adjuncts with increases in title and pay tied to the adjunct faculty development program, and due to the institution's relationship with the local school district, adjuncts earned retirement and were vested after 10 years (Phillips, 2000).

At larger institutions, not as much was offered, probably due to logistics and cost. However, there were some institutions that provided more than the average amenities. For example, Maricopa Community College District (10 campuses and two skills centers) with nearly 200,000 credit students, provided up to $500.00 per year for adjunct-specific staff and professional development funds. Adjuncts also have received tuition waivers on any Maricopa campus (Phillips, 2000).

In Virginia, educators from many higher education circles collaborated and created the Virginia Tidewater Consortium for Higher Education, funded originally by the Kellogg Foundation and later by the Pew Charitable Trusts for two years. Classes were offered on Friday afternoons and Saturdays up to four times per semester. Participants, both full- and part-time, received no stipend nor did they ask for one. Faculty were charged a nominal fee for breakfasts and lunches, and the program was often filled to capacity. Topics were limited to enhancing teaching and learning and focused on immediately useable hand-on ideas, which the participants applauded. It was noted that enthusiastic administrative support was paramount for this type of arrangement to have been successful (Dotolo, 1999).

Valencia Community College provides a year-round online orientation program to their faculty (both full- and part-time), with a stipend for completion. They also offer extensive program opportunities for professional development at various times throughout the year for both full- and part-time faculty as well. Finally, they provide all part-time faculty with email access and training so as to facilitate communication within and between departments and instructors.

Summary and Conclusions

If institutions align what occurs in the faculty development program with what instructors need and desire, and offer it when convenient, more faculty might get involved. When institutions are successful at getting more instructors involved, it will help the faculty improve their instruction, which, in turn, will ultimately improve their students' learning—the original goal (Barr & Tagg, 1995). It is up to the institution to make the commitment to their part-time faculty to better involve and integrate them into the culture of the institution to ensure their further commitment to the students. Connecting the part-time faculty to the college will further enhance the part-time faculty commitment to the college and provide for a better teaching/learning environment for the entire community.

References

Alfano, K. (1993). ERIC review: Recent strategies for faculty and staff development. *Community College Review, 21*(1), 68–77.

American Association of Community Colleges. (1997). *National profile of community colleges: Trends & statistics* (3rd ed.). Washington, DC: Author.

Anderson, S. E. (1990). The status of faculty development programs in community colleges in the state of Washington (Doctoral dissertation, University of Washington, 1989). *Dissertation Abstracts International, 51,* 720.

Bach, P. (1999, Spring). Part-time faculty are here to stay. *Planning for Higher Education, 27*(3), 32–40.

Barr, R. G., & Tagg, J. (1995, November/December). From teaching to learning—a new paradigm for undergraduate education. *Change, 27*(6), 13–25.

Board of Regents of State Colleges et al. v. Roth, 92 S. Ct. 2701 (1972).

Burnstad, H. (2000, October 22). *Adjunct faculty development.* Paper presented at the Info-Tec Workshop Series, Jacksonville, FL.

Burnstad, H. (2003). Part-time faculty development at Johnson County Community College. In G. E. Watts (Ed.), *New directions for community colleges: No. 120. Enhancing community colleges through professional development* (pp. 17–25). San Francisco, CA: Jossey-Bass.

Byrd, A. M. (1986). Four dimensions of staff development activities as related to part-time community college instructor's needs, awareness and levels of participation (Doctoral dissertation, University of Florida, 1985). *Dissertation Abstracts International, 46,* 2535.

Caffey, D. (1978). Perceptions of full-time faculty members at selected Texas public community-junior colleges regarding faculty development goals and practices (Doctoral dissertation, Texas Tech University, 1978). *Dissertation Abstracts International, 40,* 692.

Commission on the Future of Community Colleges. (1988). *Building communities: A vision for a new century.* Washington, DC: American Association of Community and Junior Colleges.

Cox, A. M. (2000, December 1). Study shows colleges' dependence on their part-time instructors: Report documents the low pay and lack of benefits for those off the tenure track. *Chronicle of Higher Education,* p. A12.

Denman, S. (1986). Role prescriptions of part-time faculty in community colleges: A comparison of interpretations of role prescriptions of part-time faculty held by part-time faculty and department chairs in community colleges. *Dissertation Abstracts International, 47,* 1994.

Dotolo, L. G. (1999). Faculty development: Working together to improve teaching and learning. In L. G. Dotolo & J. T. Strandness (Eds.), *New directions for higher education: No. 106. Best practices in higher education consortia: How institutions can work together* (pp. 51–57). San Francisco, CA: Jossey-Bass.

Gaff, J., & Morstain, B. (1978). Evaluating the outcomes. In J. G. Gaff (Ed.), *Institutional renewal through improvement of teaching* (pp. 80–96). San Francisco, CA: Jossey-Bass.

Gappa, J. M., & Leslie, D. W. (1993). *The invisible faculty: Improving the status of part-timers in higher education.* San Francisco, CA: Jossey-Bass.

Gerity, P. (1999). A study to identify community college workforce training and development professionals' perceived competencies and their perceived professional development needs (Doctoral dissertation, The Pennsylvania State University, 1999). *Dissertation Abstracts International, 60,* 2344.

Grant, M. R. (2000). Faculty development in publicly supported two-year colleges (Doctoral dissertation, Southern Illinois University Carbondale, 2000). *Dissertation Abstracts International, 61,* 209.

Katz, J., & Henry, M. (1988). *Turning professors into teachers: A new approach to faculty development and student learning.* New York, NY: Macmillan.

Klenk, M. (1996). The development needs of part-time faculty as perceived by part-time faculty and higher education administrators (Doctoral dissertation, West Virginia University, 1995). *Dissertation Abstracts International, 56,* 3017.

Leatherman, C. (2000a, November 17). Teaching assistants and universities plot strategy in union battle: NLRB ruling sets the stage for new round of organizing drives. *Chronicle of Higher Education,* p. A18.

Leatherman, C. (2000b, December 1). Union organizers propose code of university conduct: Colleges will be pushed to uphold fair labor practices. *Chronicle of Higher Education,* p. A16.

Leatherman, C. (2001, January 26). Part-time faculty members try to organize nationally: Many think the time is ripe to improve their pay and working conditions. *Chronicle of Higher Education,* p. A12.

Leslie, D. W., & Gappa, J. M. (2002). Part-time faculty: Competent and committed. In C. L. Outcalt (Ed.), *New directions for community colleges: No. 118. Community college faculty: Characteristics, practices, and challenges* (pp. 59–67). San Francisco, CA: Jossey-Bass.

Leslie, D. W., Kellams, S. E., & Gunne, G. M. (1982). *Part-time faculty in American higher education.* New York, NY: Praeger.

Lyons, R. E. (1996). A study of the effects of a mentoring initiative on the performance of new adjunct community college faculty (Doctoral dissertation, University of Central Florida, 1996). *Dissertation Abstracts International, 57,* 4243.

Maguire, P. (1983, Winter). Enhancing the effectiveness of adjunct faculty. *Community College Review, 11,* 27–33.

Miller, R. I., Finley, C., & Vancko, C. S. (2000). *Evaluating, improving, and judging faculty performance in two-year colleges.* Westport, CT: Begin & Garvey.

Moe, J. (1977). A staff development model for part-time instructors. In T. O'Banion (Ed.), *New directions for community colleges: No. 19. Developing staff potential* (pp. 35–46). San Francisco, CA: Jossey-Bass.

Naparsteck, M. (1991, September 4). Letter to editor: Part-time professors: Academe's untouchables. *Chronicle of Higher Education,* p. B6.

Perry v. Sinderman, 408 U.S. 593 (1972).

Phillips, K. (2000). *Report of faculty development in community colleges across the nation* (Internship report). Orlando, FL: Valencia Community College, Department of Curriculum, Teaching, and Learning.

Piasta, B. (1991). Staff development needs of New Jersey community college part-time faculty: Perceptions of part-time faculty, department chairs and administrators (Doctoral dissertation, Temple University, 1991). *Dissertation Abstracts International, 57,* 2356.

Rhodes, J. (1991). *A study of institutional needs of part-time faculty at Northwestern Michigan College* (Master's thesis, Ferris State University, 1991). (ERIC Document Reproduction Service No. ED346942)

Richardson, R. (1992, Summer). The associate program: Teaching improvement for adjunct faculty. *Community College Review, 20,* 29–34.

Roark, D. B. (1989). Inservice faculty development needs of part-time faculty as perceived by part-time faculty and their supervisors at three selected community colleges in Florida (Doctoral dissertation, Florida State University, 1988). *Dissertation Abstracts International, 49,* 1657.

Roueche, J. E., Roueche, S. D., & Milliron, M. D. (1995). *Strangers in their own land: Part-time faculty in American community colleges.* Washington, DC: Community College Press.

Smallwood, S. (2003, May 9). Non-tenure-track faculty members vote to unionize at U. of Michigan. *Chronicle of Higher Education,* p. A15.

Sparks, G. (1983). Synthesis of research on staff development for effective teaching. *Educational Leadership, 41*(3), 65–72.

Tinto, V. (1998, July 16). *A seminar with Vincent Tinto.* Paper presented at Valencia Community College-East Campus, Orlando, FL.

Tuck, G. (1981). Perceived staff development needs of part-time occupational technical instructors in the Virginia community college system (Doctoral dissertation, Virginia Polytechnic Institute and State University, 1981). *Dissertation Abstracts International, 42,* 977A.

Wien, S. (2002). Part-time work and self-identity: A case study of adjuncts in higher education (Doctoral dissertation, Rutgers The State University of New Jersey–New Brunswick, 2002). *Dissertation Abstracts International, 63,* 10A.

Wyles, B. (1998). Adjunct faculty in the community college: Realities and challenges. In D. W. Leslie (Ed.), *New directions for higher education: No. 104. The growing use of part-time faculty: Understanding causes and effects* (pp. 89–93). San Francisco, CA: Jossey-Bass.

PART TWO

Recruiting and Retaining Part-Time Faculty

5 | ONE FACULTY: HIRING PRACTICES AND ORIENTATION

Joseph L. Gadberry and Helen Burnstad

Adjunct faculty are a valuable resource in helping today's colleges meet their instructional mission (Greive & Worden, 2000), and adjunct faculty are a critical asset in the college work force (Gappa & Leslie, 1993). Today, adjunct faculty teach over 40% of all community college courses (Wickun & Stanley, 2003). Greive and Worden confirm and extend this finding by reporting that adjunct faculty teach between 30%–50% of all credit courses and between 95%–100% of all noncredit courses. Colleges are hiring an increasingly larger number of adjunct faculty to teach students (Cox, 2000; Leatherman, 2000). If current trends continue Lieberman and Guskin (2002) report that adjunct faculty will far surpass full-time faculty across higher education.

The need for adjunct faculty is great. As tight fiscal constraints and enrollment pressures increase, community colleges will need to depend on adjunct faculty to meet demands for instructional resources. In fact, today's limited budgets and growing community college enrollments provide new momentum for the need to understand, value, and most importantly, integrate adjunct faculty into the college community.

The purpose of this chapter is to identify and discuss specific hiring and orientation practices for adjunct faculty. In an effort to provide both the philosophical underpinnings and the pragmatics for hiring and orientating adjunct faculty, the authors have chosen to include specific examples of resources from their campus. Throughout, the reader will be invited to turn to specific resources at the end of this chapter. These resources provide specific examples of the authors' commitment to best practices in hiring and orienting adjunct faculty at Johnson County Community College (JCCC). They represent resources developed by the Office of Staff and Organizational Development, the Department of Science, and the Adjunct Training Certification Program at JCCC.

Hiring Practices

Hiring new faculty is one of the most important job responsibilities of the division/department chair. The responsibility to hire adjunct faculty is no less a priority to academic leaders than the responsibility for hiring full-time faculty. When adjunct faculty teach 50%–60% of college courses and students, hiring practices for adjunct faculty should not be compromised.

Academic leaders should establish sound hiring practices for hiring *all* college faculty. Systems and best practices in hiring adjunct faculty should be no less thoughtful and rigorous than the practices associated with hiring full-time faculty. These best practices in hiring adjunct faculty should not stray from prescribed processes even in emergencies when an instructor is needed to staff an unstaffed course section at the last minute. One can appreciate the need to meet student demand, but one must also be dedicated to the importance of maintaining high standards in the process and outcomes of hiring adjunct faculty. The standards and credibility with which adjunct faculty are hired will have a direct impact on perceptions of professionalism for adjunct faculty, department/division chairs, full-time faculty, and ultimately on the campus at large.

Learning should be the primary focus in the classroom. Hiring full- or part-time faculty who are qualified to facilitate learning must be the goal of academic leaders. Academic chairs/division leaders must hire full- and part-time faculty who possess a teaching style that engages students in the learning process, are committed to providing the students with a quality education, exhibit an enthusiasm for their discipline, demonstrate a contagious attitude toward learning, and encourage the students to be successful.

The goal of each college should be to integrate full- and part-time faculty into one faculty. One faculty comprised of full- and part-time staff dedicated to learning and student success can only be achieved through careful recruiting, selection, and orientation practices built into the college/division/department hiring practices. In order to achieve this integration of faculty positions, academic leaders must be dedicated to recruiting and selecting the very best adjunct faculty possible. Equally important, leaders must integrate adjunct faculty into their division/department through orientation processes that enculturate, include, and celebrate the contributions of adjunct faculty within the college culture.

Recruitment of new adjunct faculty should be directed toward addressing identified needs within the division/department. Employing new faculty whose qualifications and professional demeanor complement the skills and attributes of full-time faculty members who teach in the department is critical. New part-time faculty members should possess professional breadth and depth of knowledge in their respective disciplines, willingness to develop best practices in teaching, and support the goals of the designated department/division and college.

Posting and Recruitment

Recruitment and posting for adjunct faculty positions should take into consideration the course, student, and department needs. Postings for part-time faculty need to be aligned with the teaching expectations of full-time faculty. Preparing a position description for adjunct professors articulates competencies and clarifies expectations for adjunct faculty. In addition, the position description offers a foundation for professionalism that allows all members of the campus community— faculty, staff, and students—to understand and appreciate the professional requirements and standards to which adjunct faculty are held. Credibility, respect, and inclusion within the campus culture for adjunct faculty can only occur when all campus constituencies see that the standards for adjunct faculty are clearly articulated, rigorous, and parallel to the professional standards for full-time faculty.

Designing a posting for a specific adjunct faculty position within a department/division is the next step in the hiring process. Pay attention to details when designing a posting. Be sure to include requests for the academic degrees that are required for teaching, previous teaching experience, computer literacy, as well as the ability to demonstrate fluency in written and oral communication. Figure 5.1 is an example of a discipline-specific posting for an adjunct faculty member. Note that responsibilities, qualifications, requests for transcripts, and position status are all included on the posting.

In addition to the specific information provided in Figure 5.1, a posting can identify the college's accrediting agency requirements for

FIGURE 5.1
SAMPLE JOB POSTING FOR CHEMISTRY

Adjunct Assistant Professor—Chemistry

Responsibilities

Instruct students in chemistry lecture and/or laboratory courses.

Qualifications

Master's degree in chemistry required. Doctorate in chemistry preferred. One-year of college-level teaching experience in chemistry required. Three years of community college teaching experience preferred. Successful candidate will be able to demonstrate computer literacy and familiarity with the use of appropriate computer software and be able to demonstrate fluency in written and oral communications.

Please submit unofficial transcript(s) of all post–secondary education with application. If employed, certified transcripts for all college-level education will be required.

Position Status

Part-time, temporary, fall 2005 semester. Variable hours and days.

educational training for classroom teachers. The posting can also identify teaching responsibilities and list days and times that the class meets, when applicable.

A request for unofficial transcripts should be included in the posting as they can provide valuable information for the hiring process, such as the applicant's academic background as it relates to the position being filled. Adjunct faculty will often apply for full-time faculty positions within the same department. Therefore, the educational requirements for adjunct faculty should reflect the educational requirements for full-time faculty. Thus, when adjuncts apply for full-time teaching positions in their department they will possess the appropriate educational background and training expected of full-time faculty.

Many college human resource departments list their open adjunct faculty teaching positions on their college web sites. To increase the pool of applicants, request that the posting also be advertised in local newspapers and job fairs. Send the posting to local high schools and universities. Graduate students in doctoral degree programs at area colleges and high school teachers are often eager to teach in the community college setting.

Preparing a careful position description and posting for adjunct faculty positions is a critical first step in hiring adjunct faculty who will understand the professional competencies and requirements of the part-time teaching position. The position description and posting are also important documents for others within the campus community as well. Members of the campus community are more likely to include and appreciate adjunct faculty when they understand the professional standards to which adjunct faculty are held.

Screening and Interview

The next stage of the hiring and orienting process is the screening and interview process. All applicants should be screened according to the requirements and qualifications listed in the job posting. When screening applicants, use an applicant evaluation grid that lists each of the required and preferred qualifications. Table 5.1 provides specific examples of screening criteria.

Table 5.1
Adjunct Screening Application Evaluation Grid

Applicant Evaluation Grid
CHEMISTRY
Posting Number
Bold skills are required

Name	Master's in chemistry	1 year teaching in academic setting	Unofficial transcript and cover letter	Computer literacy	Fluency in written and oral communication skills	Ability to work as part of instructional team	Willingness to participate in all program-related activities	Ph.D. preferred	3 years teaching experience in academic setting preferred	Teaching in a community college preferred	Ongoing professional development preferred	Comments

While many campuses allow the department/division head to interview and select adjunct faculty, interview teams or selection committees to interview the applicants who meet qualifications of the posting should be used as well. The composition of this committee should include at least one person who teaches in the discipline for which the applicant is being interviewed, one other faculty member (full-time or adjunct), and the department head. The interview committee for the science department at JCCC consists of the assistant dean (department head), adjunct liaison, and at least one faculty member from the discipline for which the applicant is interviewing. Use a common set of questions for all applicants. If the Department of

Human Resources does not provide a screening and interview form, create a form that can be used. Maintain careful records of all applicants for each position posted. To prevent litigious situations, carefully use the application evaluation grids and qualification screening during the screening for interview process.

A teaching demonstration during the interview allows members of the selection team to assess the applicant's teaching style and competencies. The interview process should include a 10–15 minute teaching demonstration in order to provide the interview team with an opportunity to view the applicant in an abbreviated teaching setting, observe the applicant's teaching style, and determine his or her familiarity, currency, and accuracy with the course content. The topic of the teaching demonstration can be assigned at the time the interview is scheduled.

When one contacts the applicant for the adjunct faculty teaching position, explain the interview process and ask if the interviewee prefers to give the teaching demonstration at the beginning or after the question and answer portion of the interview. During the question and answers segment of the interview, encourage the interviewee to share specific work or classroom experiences in an effort to understand more about the interviewee's past experiences and potential as an adjunct faculty member in the department.

Prior to hire, contact at least one person who has observed the applicant in the classroom, if the applicant has had prior teaching experience. Preferably, contact an immediate supervisor, department chair, or other instructional officer as a reference. If the applicant has had no prior teaching experience, contact a supervisor for a reference regarding potential for teaching effectiveness. References are an important resource in the hiring process and can provide valuable information about classroom performance; ability to work with students, faculty, and coworkers; reliability, and the ability to follow college policies and procedures. It is always advisable to contact the applicant's immediate and/or past supervisors rather than personal references. If the supervisor gives an unfavorable account of the applicant's teaching performance, check with other past supervisors to affirm or refute the most recent supervisor's comments.

During the interview process, provide the applicant with a copy of the course outline and course competencies for the course(s) to be taught. The interview is the appropriate time to explain teaching and classroom expectations. Clarify what you expect of the faculty. Figure 5.2 provides a listing of important considerations. Clarifying policies and procedures, expectations, and professional development during the interview will open communication and provide opportunities to ensure that the candidate understands expectations for employment as an adjunct faculty member. Help the interviewee understand what they can expect from students, faculty, their supervisor, and the college. Review the course teaching load, including days and times that classes meet, with the applicant. Figure 5.3 provides a specific outline of key issues to be discussed during the interview and hiring process. This list offers the interviewing committee and the applicant a snapshot of important information including phone and Internet details, copy center location, and so on.

Explain the college policy on course reimbursement, including pay raises and pay for substitute teaching. JCCC uses a sliding scale to pay adjuncts based on degree (bachelor's, master's, specialist, and doctorate) and number of semesters they have taught at the college. All adjunct faculty members at JCCC receive the same rate of pay increase as the full-time faculty. If a community college provides a cost of living increase to adjunct faculty, the applicant should be informed of this.

Adjunct faculty frequently request more classes or a larger workload than college policy allows for them to teach and continue to be considered part-time; therefore, advise the applicant of the maximum number of hours that can be taught in a given term or academic year. Outline the college's policies on class absence and class cancellation. Attention to details of compensation and policies during the interview process is important to managing issues related to adjunct faculty and will open communication and clearly specify expectations and requirements at the outset of the professional relationship between the adjunct faculty member and the college. Figure 5.4 provides a summary of the many benefits and services for adjunct faculty.

According to Gappa and Leslie (1993), 85% of adjunct faculty were hired for one year or less, and 64% were hired for one term. A survey of adjunct faculty at JCCC during the 1999–2000 academic

FIGURE 5.2
WHAT ADJUNCT FACULTY NEED TO KNOW

College Policies and Procedures

- Faculty handbook
- Sick days
- Overtime
- Field trips
- Employee expectations
- Mileage
- In-class emergencies
- Procedure to determine contact hours
- Substitute teaching
- Copyright laws
- Email
- College calendar with important dates
- College-wide safety

Departmental Policies and Procedures

- Administrative policies and procedures
- Contact person
- Administrative assistant
- Staff
- Discipline/content contact
- Course Materials
- Curriculum
- Course prerequisites and co-requisites
- Course competencies
- Course syllabus
- Field trips
- Expectation of faculty and students
- Mailbox and email addresses
- Classroom location
- Resources for faculty
- Class rosters

- Procurement of texts, supplies, keys
- Office hours and office space
- Grading and evaluation of students
- Copy machine access
- Computer availability for adjuncts
- Safety procedures
- Opportunities for adjunct involvement with full-time faculty

Student Services Policies and Procedures

- Registration
- Add/drop policies
- Grade change
- Attendance
- Student code of conduct
- Student behavior
- Student cheating
- Classroom management
- Student resources (including tutors)
- Documentation issues

Professional Development

- Test construction
- Library resources and media
- Teaching and learning process
- Student assessment and evaluation
- Distance learning
- Technology in the classroom
- Student instruction

Know Your Audience

- Begin at the beginning
- Teach to competencies of the course
- Meet students where they are
- Tell students what is expected of them

FIGURE 5.3

JCCC SCIENCE DEPARTMENT INTERVIEW AND PRESENTATION FORM

JCCC Science Department

Interview for:

Presentation topic: Concept of the Mole

August 6, 2003

- Adjunct liaison: Dr. X
- Adjunct orientation and workshop: August 14, 2003, 4:45 p.m., CLB 312
- Safety workshop:
- Lead instruction: Dr. X
- Outline of course competencies that are required to be taught: http://web.jccc.net/academic/science/courses/index.html
- CASE classroom: CLB 112
- Office, telephone, and email:
- Document services: CSB 161
- Copy center: LIB 226
- Tuition reimbursement after two semesters of teaching at JCCC:
- Absences: two hours per contract hour per course (= two weeks spring/fall; one week summer) without penalty
- Life Fitness Center:
- Children's Center (upon availability):
- Staff development courses:
- Adjunct Certificate Training (ACT): $800 stipend upon completion
- Staff discounts available for many performances in Yardley Hall, The Theater, Recital Hall, and the Black Box Theater
- Course compensation/workload hour taught: $718 per workload hour x five hours = $3,950 for one lecture section of CHEM I
- Substitution pay: $27.50/hour
- Class schedule: TR 11:00–12:50 p.m. on MTWRF in room SCI 114

FIGURE 5.4
ADJUNCT BENEFITS

Johnson County Community College offers many benefits and services to the adjunct staff. These include:

- Tuition reimbursement for an employee and dependents taking JCCC credit classes is available after two semesters of teaching. An example of an application form is included and further information is available in the Office of Human Resources (GEB 251).
- Adjunct faculty who teach classes for 15 weeks plus one final exam week may receive two paid hours of absence per hour taught during one regular week. For example, a faculty member teaching three hours per week during the 16-week semester may receive up to six hours of paid absence during the semester. For shorter classes (e.g., summer school), absences will be prorated based on the regular 16-week semester.
- FICA (Social Security) contribution
- Workers' compensation insurance
- Liability insurance
- Voluntary tax sheltered annuity participation
- A variety of professional development opportunities
- Use of the JCCC Life Fitness Center. Further information is available from the Physical Education Division (GYM 103) or at http://www.jccc.net/home/depts.php/4634
- Children's Center (upon availability; a fee is charged). See http://www.jccc.net/home/depts.php/9104
- Free tickets to performances by the Academic Theatre Department
- Representation on the Adjunct Advisory Council, which meets with the vice president of instruction
- Voice mailboxes and email accounts
- See the brochures relating to adjunct benefits in the Office of Staff and Organizational Development (GEB 238)

year found that 43% of respondents indicated that it was very important for them to attain permanent status as a JCCC employee. Of
those responding to the survey, 30% were waiting for a full-time position at JCCC, 20% said they were actively seeking employment outside of the college, and 29% replied that they were satisfied to only
teach part-time. Since many applicants are looking for job security, it
is advisable to inform them at the time of the interview that the position is temporary. Inform new hires on adjunct teaching opportunities
beyond the first temporary contract. At JCCC, adjuncts are not
required to reapply for successive semesters of teaching, but their contracts are temporary contracts.

Although many adjunct faculty desire health care benefits, very
few community colleges provide health insurance or retirement benefits for the adjunct faculty (Gappa & Leslie, 1993). At the time of the
interview, provide the applicants with a brief orientation to the college
and department, and inform them of existing adjunct benefits including availability of health insurance or retirement plans, if any.
Professional development opportunities including availability of travel
funds for professional development/discipline-related meetings, discounts for college sponsored musical and theatrical performances, and
tuition reimbursement are some of the other benefits in which adjunct
faculty may be interested. Adjunct faculty will also want to know about
the availability of classroom and office resources including audiovisual
and technology services, email, voicemail, mailbox, and office supplies.
Figure 5.5 summarizes detailed information to finalize the applicant
as an adjunct faculty member.

Emphasize the importance of attending adjunct orientation and
other special workshops including lab safety training or other discipline-specific training sessions. It is good to provide a personalized
written copy of this information to the applicant at the conclusion of
the interview. Follow up with an official letter of invitation to the
adjunct orientation and include a brief description of the planned
activities for the orientation.

Hiring qualified adjunct faculty is the first step in building a
teaching team that perceives itself as one faculty. The foregoing
processes of including full-time faculty in the adjunct hiring process,
explicit selection criteria, and hiring systems that are open and com-

FIGURE 5.5
SCIENCE DEPARTMENT NEW-HIRE CHECKLIST

Name_____

SS #_____

Degree/Rate_____

Board Approval Date_____

- ☐ Copy application and place in hanging folder
- ☐ Make new hanging file folder
- ☐ Make mailbox label
- ☐ Rolodex card
- ☐ Supplemental contract
- ☐ Salary to spreadsheet
- ☐ Fax first page of the application to the vice president of instruction to process the instructor into BANNER
- ☐ Input name on "G" drive folder for board approval
- ☐ Insert instructor name in BANNER
- ☐ Create workload form
- ☐ In-service contract
- ☐ Web page update

municative provide the foundation for credibility, inclusion, and acceptance of adjunct faculty within the college culture.

Orientation

Help assimilate and integrate new adjunct faculty into the college community by providing comprehensive orientation experiences. Orientation needs to include strategies to open communication and affirm the department and college philosophy that adjunct faculty are important members of the teaching staff. At the time of hire, provide the adjunct faculty member with copies of all teaching materials including sample syllabus, textbooks, transparencies, solution manuals, appropriate software and test banks needed to teach the assigned classes, as well as a copy of the faculty handbook, college catalog, and other materials that will help introduce the adjunct faculty member to the college. If the institution has the college catalog, faculty handbook, and course outlines available only online, provide the web sites where these documents can be found. Direct the new hire to fill out all necessary paperwork and documents in human resources, including payroll documents, prior to their first day of classes. These routine tasks of orientation are critical and will facilitate understanding of human resources and teaching processes on your campus.

An induction checklist helps to identify the tasks that need to be completed prior to the beginning of classes, such as identifying office space and providing keys/access cards for office space, classrooms and mailroom, parking permit, telephone extension/voice mailbox, computer access and email address, add to listservs and/or distribution lists, business cards, note pads, and office supplies (see Figure 5.5).

Adjunct orientation is the time to officially welcome adjunct faculty to campus and to transition them into the academic culture of the college. Adjunct orientation needs to be rich with information necessary for success in teaching and learning. Information about safety issues, field trips, absences, employee expectations, attendance policies, computer access and email, substitute teaching, mailboxes, photocopying, and how to obtain supplies are all issues to be discussed during orientation.

While providing needed information is central to adjunct orientations, it is also important to communicate key cultural values and attitudes about faculty, students, and the college culture at the time of your adjunct orientation. Several different types of adjunct orientations have been initiated by different community colleges. One community college refers to their orientation as the Adjunct Extravaganza. Cultural values associated with acceptance and inclusion are clearly inherent in this orientation. Central Michigan University has online adjunct orientations. Again, values regarding the effective use of technology are included in the orientation. A college may elect to have a centralized or decentralized orientation. Published resources provided during orientation may include handouts, resource books, teaching tips and tools, videos or CDs. The variety of formats and resources is rich and diverse. However, regardless of format, orientation is a critical time to share important information and cultural values.

Orientation Model

JCCC holds a comprehensive orientation for all new adjuncts and provides a refresher orientation for adjuncts that have taught at the college for seven or more semesters. The adjunct faculty orientation activities are held on the Thursday prior to the beginning of classes in the fall and spring semesters. All new adjuncts are invited to attend this orientation sponsored by the Office of Staff and Organizational Development. The purpose of this centralized orientation is threefold.

First, the orientation welcomes newly hired adjuncts to JCCC. It provides the venue for sharing resource materials about JCCC and employment at the college. Importantly, the orientation also creates an environment for community building. Adjunct faculty, full-time faculty, chairs, deans, and members of the JCCC administration have the opportunity to meet and engage in conversations. The JCCC New Faculty Orientation begins at 6 p.m. with a buffet dinner for all newly hired adjunct and full-time faculty. Adjunct liaisons, assistant deans, and deans also attend. The director for staff and organization development facilitates the orientation, and the vice presidents for instruction and student services provide brief greetings.

All new adjunct faculty members receive an orientation information packet. This packet includes information about the college, training and development programs offered through the Office of Staff and Organizational Development, a who's who in support services (a list of names to contact in the different support services on campus), a reminder from human resources to turn in an official transcript, and information on document services. The packet also includes information and publications on teaching tips, Adjunct Certification Training, student demographics, and adjunct faculty benefits. The orientation lasts one hour. In accordance with college procedures, all adjuncts that attend orientation meetings prior to the dinner and after the dinner are paid for their attendance. The rate of pay for attendance at adjunct orientation meetings has been established as the same rate of pay as adjunct and full-time faculty receive for substitute teaching.

Following the dinner, adjunct faculty members adjourn to the decentralized department-specific adjunct meetings. These meetings include returning and newly hired adjunct faculty members. These meetings provide all adjuncts within a department/discipline with an opportunity to meet together as a faculty and to receive specific information for them to have a successful semester.

Science Department Model

All newly hired adjuncts attend a discipline-specific orientation meeting led by the adjunct liaison prior to the college-sponsored buffet dinner. The adjunct liaison is a full-time faculty member who has partial reassigned time for the specific purpose of facilitating knowledge, information, and professional growth for the adjunct faculty members in the department. This discipline-specific orientation is formatted as a group orientation to meet the specific needs of the newly hired science adjuncts. The adjunct liaison for the sciences reviews college and departmental policies and procedures to assist their transition into the academic culture of the science faculty. The adjunct liaison answers questions and gives relevant applications that will reinforce the policies and procedures.

At this time, new adjunct faculty receive copies of the *Science Department Faculty Handbook,* a *Tips Flip Chart,* and the *Science Department Adjunct Orientation* on a CD. The *Tips Flip Chart* is an orientation in a nutshell, with names and extensions for adjunct support and student support. This resource also tells the new adjunct how to enter grades electronically and has a to-do list that indicates actions the adjunct faculty member must complete prior to the first week of class, at the beginning of the semester, and during the semester. The *Tips Flip Chart* and *Science Department Adjunct Orientation* CD are modeled after similar products used at Frederick Community College.

The CD provides the adjunct faculty members the opportunity to carry the disc with them and refer to it as the need arises. The disc provides an individualized approach to orientation to the department and college. The vice presidents of instruction and student services, directors of staff and organizational development, the Center for Teaching and Learning (CTL), library, enrollment management, educational technology center, divisional dean, assistant dean (instructional officer for science department), administrative assistant for the sciences, and the adjunct liaison for the sciences are introduced to the adjunct faculty through cameo appearances on the CD. The disc has a PowerPoint presentation on the details of being an adjunct faculty member in the department and benefits that are available to adjuncts at JCCC. The disc links to important web sites on campus including the college catalog, faculty handbook, student services, human resources, and science department. Links to important academic forms that the adjunct will use during the semester are also incorporated in this electronic document. Adjunct faculty members are given a brief overview of the science department through a five-minute video that is incorporated into the disc. The disc is close captioned for the hearing impaired.

Following the new adjunct faculty dinner, the recently hired science adjuncts are introduced at the science department's faculty meeting for all science department adjuncts (decentralized orientation). Again, refreshments are provided. The meeting is planned and facilitated by the science department adjunct liaison. This time is used for staff and professional development activities and training. A content expert (college employee or external consultant) is invited to facilitate professional development activities such as active learning in the college classroom, how to use pipeline, unlawful harassment, and use of WebCT in the classroom. The goal of this discipline-specific orientation is to provide meaningful teaching and learning resources for adjunct faculty.

The science department also holds an adjunct orientation for newly hired adjuncts that teach during the summer semester. The adjuncts again receive the informational packets from the Office of Staff and Organizational Development. This orientation is modeled after the group orientation held for new science adjunct faculty in the fall and spring semesters, and supplemental contracts are issued to all attendees. Once again, the newly hired adjunct faculty are served dinner and invited to engage in conversations about teaching and learning in a process designed to build community among all faculty at JCCC.

Adjunct Liaison

Community colleges employ large numbers of adjunct faculty. This can become a management issue for the department chair/head. JCCC recognized this problem and established an adjunct instructor facilitator position in the math department in 1992, in the science department in 1993, and in other departments across campus during the last decade. The job description is formalized campus-wide. Gadberry and DiCostanzo (1995) and Gadberry (1996) describe the adjunct facilitator as a faculty member who assists with the management of adjunct faculty. This position is now called the adjunct liaison to more aptly reflect the position responsibilities. According to the JCCC adjunct liaison job description, this individual is a liaison between the adjunct and the assistant dean and between the adjunct faculty and full-time faculty for issues related to the classroom. Figure 5.6 identifies the responsibilities and duties of the adjunct liaison.

The faculty members who hold these positions may be full-time or adjunct faculty. Adjunct liaisons are professional peers/mentors of the adjunct faculty members and not supervisors. They receive one hour of reassigned time from classroom teaching for every eight adjunct faculty members assigned to them. The maximum number of adjuncts assigned to an adjunct liaison is 32. The larger departments employ several adjunct liaisons to accommodate the large number of adjuncts. The role of the adjunct liaison in the sciences includes assistance with screening adjunct applications and interviewing in the hiring process and coordinating fall and spring semester orientations. The adjunct liaison may serve the role of a mentor for adjunct faculty, providing a nurturing environment, and they may serve as a teaching resource for the adjunct faculty who are experiencing classroom problems that may not lead to a successful learning environment. The adjunct liaison makes classroom observations and schedules post- classroom visits with the assistant dean. The adjunct liaison attends the post-classroom observation with the adjunct faculty member and the assistant dean and reviews the observation with the faculty member, providing constructive comments, and when appropriate, giving recommendations that would help the adjunct be more successful in the classroom.

According to Smith and Wright (2000), adjunct faculty are an important resource in helping the college meet its instructional mission. Adjunct faculty members need to be treated accordingly.

FIGURE 5.6
ADJUNCT FACULTY LIAISON POSITION DESCRIPTION

I. Position Title: Adjunct Liaison

II. Reports to: Assistant Dean

Position Description

The adjunct liaison serves as liaison for the adjunct faculty, assistant dean, and full-time faculty for academic issues related to the classroom.

Major Position Responsibilities

The adjunct liaison acts as a liaison for the assistant dean, full-time faculty, and adjunct faculty in curriculum-related issues. The adjunct liaison will facilitate communication among members of the department and help integrate adjunct faculty into the college community.

At the discretion of the assistant dean, the adjunct liaison may:

- Assist with staffing class schedules with adjunct faculty.
- Screen applications for part-time teaching positions and help interview adjunct applications.
- Assist with adjunct classroom observations and schedule follow-up meetings (when appropriate with the assistant dean). File observation reports with the assistant dean.
- Assist with preparation of reports relating to adjunct faculty.
- Assist with facilitation of adjunct responsibilities (i.e., textbooks, course syllabi and outlines, student evaluation procedures, colloquiums, and questions related to policies and procedures of the department/program, division, and college).
- Provide a forum for increasing communication and dissemination of information.
- Bring forth adjunct faculty concerns when appropriate, and assist with awards and recognition of adjunct faculty.
- Attend discipline-related meetings.
- Coordinate the teaching materials of adjunct instructors, ensuring that adjunct teachers have all necessary materials.
- Mentor adjunct faculty regarding course preparation, presentation, and testing.

At the discretion of the assistant dean, the adjunct liaison may coordinate:

- Textbook orders.
- Adjunct orientation and in-service activities, including follow-up sessions.
- The preparation, organization, distribution, collection, and grading of the departmental final for introductory courses.
- The development of pre-test/post-test models for introductory courses.

Assignment and distribution of hours for the adjunct liaison position will be at the discretion of the assistant dean, consistent with college policy.

Summary and Conclusions

Adjunct faculty members are a needed and valued instructional resource for today's colleges. Attention to process and details in hiring and orienting adjunct faculty will reap benefits for the college, the department, and the adjunct faculty member. Hiring for excellence and orienting adjunct faculty into the campus culture with important information, open communication, and effective teaching and learning strategies will facilitate a community of faculty (full-time and part-time) where value, acceptance, and inclusion lead to one faculty dedicated to student learning outcomes and student success.

References

Cox, A. M. (2000, December 1). Study shows colleges' dependence on their part-time instructors: Report documents the low pay and lack of benefits for those off the tenure track. *Chronicle of Higher Education*, p. A12.

Gadberry, J. (1996). The adjunct faculty instructor facilitator. *Academic Leadership*, 4(1), 10–12.

Gadberry, J., & DiCostanzo, J. (1995). Improving adjunct faculty competence and longevity. *The Department Chair*, 6(2), 13–14.

Gappa, J. M., & Leslie, D. W. (1993). *The invisible faculty. Improving the status of part-timers in higher education.* San Francisco, CA: Jossey-Bass.

Greive, D. E., & Worden, C. A. (Eds.). (2000). *Managing adjunct & part-time faculty for the new millennium.* Elyria, OH: Info-Tec.

Leatherman, C. (2000, January 28). Part-timers continue to replace full-timers on college faculties: Education department report says adjuncts now make up nearly half the professoriate. *Chronicle of Higher Education*, p. A18.

Lieberman, D., & Guskin, A. (2002). The essential role of faculty development in higher education. In C. M. Wehlburg & S. Chadwick-Blossey (Eds.), *To improve the academy: Vol. 21. Resources for faculty, instructional, and organizational development* (pp. 257–271). Bolton, MA: Anker.

Smith, M., & Wright, D. (2000). Orientation of adjunct and part-time faculty—exemplary models. In D. E. Greive & C. A. Worden (Eds.), *Managing adjunct & part-time faculty for the new millennium* (pp. 45–69). Elyria, OH: Info-Tec.

Wickun, W. G., & Stanley, R. F. (2003). *The role of adjunct faculty in higher education.* Retrieved October 14, 2003, from http://mtprof.msun.edu/Win2000/Wickun.html

6 | The Challenge and Effective Use of Part-Time Faculty

Alice W. Villadsen and Thomas I. Anderson

Since its founding in 1978, Brookhaven College has benefited from the talents of adjunct faculty. Over the years the college has attempted to improve the effectiveness of its adjunct faculty members, integrating them more fully into the larger college life for their own professional satisfaction and development and for the success of students.

This chapter will examine how Brookhaven College, an institution of approximately 11,000 credit and 5,000 non-credit students per semester, has dealt with the challenge and effective use of adjunct faculty. Adjunct faculty have been employed at Brookhaven College for 25 years and within the district for 45 years. Although practices have changed many times, new learning occurs constantly.

Part-time instructors have a long history of being crucial members of the teaching faculty in the Dallas County Community College District (DCCCD). At the conclusion of the first year of operation for El Centro College, the first of the seven DCCCD colleges, the founding chancellor, Bill Priest, reported that 89 full-time faculty and 69 part-time faculty were employed: "These [the part-timers] taught mainly in the Evening College and in the Community Service Program" (Priest, 1967). Interestingly, Dr. Priest also projected that in the second year of operations,

The Evening and Community Service programs are expected to grow dramatically. Over 200 classes (almost double the number for last fall) have been developed and approved for the community service area alone. Almost 80 classes are to be offered in the Evening College. Approximately half of the students enrolled will be taking courses in the evening.

Heavy reliance on adjunct instructors at community colleges is more than a trend; it is a way to do the business of education. Frequently, they are highly qualified, flexible, willing, and proficient at teaching. They bring immediacy and currency to the classroom for many are practitioners of what they teach. They emerge from the surrounding community and are natural fits for community-based colleges.

However, they also present special challenges. Since they come and go, often under the "cloak of darkness," how does the college connect with them? How do they get the administrative and instructional support they need? How is their effectiveness evaluated? How does the college ensure that students have access to them? How can professional development experiences be provided for them? How are they engaged in the life of the college? How are they honored? And when their ranks thin due to economic realities, burnout, or full-time opportunities, how are new ones recruited and oriented? How does the college make pay attractive enough to keep them?

Recruitment of Adjunct Faculty

A first challenge for colleges using adjunct instructors is always in recruiting them. Just as soon as a dean thinks a good, solid list of part-time faculty prospects for the coming term has been assembled, things happen to change the available pool and the needs of the division. The list of possible and interested candidates should always exceed the expected need, so a multiple approach to recruitment is essential.

Adjunct faculty members are recruited at Brookhaven in a number of ways: newspaper ads and college web sites, job fairs, and referrals by the other adjuncts and lead faculty. Experience has shown that job fairs are a good way to recruit new adjuncts, provided they are hired immediately. The later the references collected at job fairs are pursued, the more likely the prospects have found employment elsewhere. Word of mouth, though, is the most productive method, if not the most scientific or business-like. Sometimes unsolicited resumes arrive, and sometimes a dean or other hiring administrator simply follows up a good lead.

No matter how adjuncts are found, there must be a process for verifying that they are qualified to teach in the discipline through an examination of credentials: the dean or the discipline's lead faculty member reviews the applications, interviews all qualified candidates, verifies transcripts and professional experience credentials, and reviews the credentials inventory form—a listing of degrees held, graduate hours completed, courses taught at the college, and years of teaching experience.

While unofficial transcripts may be used for the interview, official transcripts are required upon hire. The dean is then responsible for noting the required graduate hours on the transcripts and verifying the degree. The careful handling of affirmation of credentials and the completed file are crucial when accrediting agencies ask for verification of faculty credentials.

Contracting and Pay

Contracts and pay methods and amounts for adjunct instructors vary from market to market. Some organizations contract with adjunct faculty by the hour. Brookhaven College has converted to a pay-by-the-course contract. Thus, a contract is based upon the number of credits (including labs) that an adjunct teaches. On the contract are listed the general responsibilities for that work. An adjunct faculty member is never contracted for more than 49% of a full-time teaching load, so on a semester basis, most adjuncts teach two credit courses or less.

Pay itself is an annual district decision. However, Brookhaven College does compete for faculty with several local universities and with two neighboring community college districts. Many adjuncts also teach for those neighboring institutions and thus cobble together a fuller teaching schedule. Of course, it is very important to maintain a pay scale for adjuncts that is adequate, if not appealing. Annually, the district reviews pay provided at neighboring institutions, an across-the-board raise is given to the adjunct contracts equivalent to the percentage raise given to full-time faculty, and tabs are kept on the difficulty that deans are having in actually hiring adjuncts. Fortunately, the Dallas area has many highly qualified potential faculty, and the economy in the early 2000s has aided in keeping a good pool of interested adjuncts. Through these formal and informal mechanisms, the college has developed a strong and loyal set of adjunct instructors who enjoy working at the college.

Orientation

Orientation for adjuncts at Brookhaven occurs at both the institutional and division levels and combines the necessities of orientation with professional development and an awards celebration at the fall convocation. The president, college administrators, deans, and full-time faculty members participate in the events, which give the adjunct faculty a better sense of connection to the college. A free dinner gives everyone a chance to socialize and the adjuncts a chance to get to know their full-time colleagues as well as one another.

For a number of years, Brookhaven provided a Saturday orientation for adjuncts. During the latter half of the 1990s, the program consisted mostly of small-group sessions based upon a variety of themes: classroom management, dealing with disruptive students, web resources, presentations about the college's resources and student support services, using email, and an introduction to the community college environment.

In 2000, the college added to this program nationally-known keynote speakers who addressed such issues as student success and learning styles. Evaluations indicated that adjuncts have appreciated this investment in and commitment to their professional development.

In addition to the college's orientation, which has served as a rally/convocation/professional development event, adjunct faculty also experience orientation within their respective divisions. While the college's orientation is a workshop, new adjuncts are introduced to the finer points of community college life through their deans and lead instructors/faculty supervisors. Typically, the various divisions have their own sessions after the large-group session.

Most division deans conduct their own orientation, and lead faculty/supervisors often follow-up on a discipline level. While each division divides responsibilities as it sees fit, usually the lead faculty member will discuss curriculum, classroom support services, educational objectives, syllabi, and pedagogical techniques—especially for those new to the community college setting. Non-instructional policies and procedures are also covered, such as record keeping and turning in grade rolls.

Support Services and Professional Development

In addition to orientation and professional development for adjunct faculty at the beginning of terms, Brookhaven College offers ongoing support in their work. All receive the *Adjunct Faculty Handbook* which outlines the college's policies, operations, expectations, and services. Mailboxes and duplication services are located in division offices, which stay open into the evening hours to provide support for evening faculty. Email and voicemail accounts are available. Audio and visual material and equipment are provided, along with access to all services in the Learning Resource Center. A Testing Center, which faculty can use to administer tests, is available with day, evening, and weekend hours.

The college's Teaching and Learning Center provides a pleasant, quiet environment where adjunct faculty can read, study, prepare materials, grade papers and tests, access their email and the Internet, work at multimedia workstations, preview videos, view teleconferences, and learn how to use educational technology. Some office space is designated for adjunct faculty as well, although the college does not provide private offices to adjuncts due to institutional crowding.

Also through the Teaching and Learning Center, adjunct instructors are invited to participate for free in the ongoing professional development courses offered through the center. These courses are usually workshops—typically an hour or two long and scheduled at convenient times, including evenings—and they cover topics from PowerPoint to Blackboard applications to student evaluation techniques. Adjuncts may take any of the classes that the Teaching and Learning Center offers each term.

Brookhaven College was fortunate to secure a Title III grant to support the college's efforts to serve a growing number of culturally and ethnically diverse students who have barriers to learning and success and to increase their retention rates. Since the project is based upon the need to provide more structure, support, and relevance in these students' learning environments, it was only logical that a component of the project focus upon the training of adjunct faculty members. A series of three workshops that are repeated several times throughout the year was developed. Supplemental pay is available for adjuncts who attend. The workshops offered are:

1) Preparing for the Critical First Three Weeks
2) Learning Patterns and Styles
3) Making Learning Work for a World of Differences: Honoring Diversity Through Teaching

The objectives for all three aim to provide useful knowledge that can make a difference in the way a faculty member conducts the class and thus positively impact student retention and success.

The first workshop—Preparing for the Critical First Three Weeks—helps adjunct faculty to identify key elements that contribute to an organized course, techniques that reduce stress levels beginning with the first day of class, ways to become acquainted with students and their needs, and how to handle latecomers and motivate students for regular attendance.

The second workshop—Learning Patterns and Styles—helps faculty members identify and learn about the elements of their own learning styles, which leads to a discussion of differences in learning styles. The adjuncts gain insight into their students' differing styles and are challenged to evaluate the effectiveness of their preferred methods of instruction and to apply what they have learned about learning differences to their teaching.

The third workshop—Making Learning Work for a World of Differences: Honoring Diversity Through Teaching—specifically addresses a phenomenon that has been growing over the past several years: the increase in minority and international student enrollments. This workshop promotes the value of diversity by informing faculty about the college's demographics and the relation of those demographics to the classroom. Similar to the second workshop, faculty members are challenged to develop instructional strategies based on diversity concepts.

Participation on the part of adjunct faculty members has been encouraging. From January 2001 to September 2003, a total of 323 adjunct faculty participants attended 22 workshops, an average of 15 per workshop. Overall participation rates for the three workshops stand between 20%–39%. Since all workshops continue to be offered, participation rates continue to climb.

A final support offered to adjunct instructors at Brookhaven College is the availability of travel funds both within divisions and at the college and district levels. With careful planning and appropriate approvals, adjunct instructors may travel to conferences and participate in other remote opportunities for professional development, an experience that is not typical of most community colleges' support options for adjuncts.

Evaluation of Adjunct Faculty

Adjunct instructors are evaluated regularly at Brookhaven College. The *Adjunct Faculty Handbook* provides both them and their supervisors with the process for evaluation. All new adjunct instructors are evaluated each semester; continuing adjuncts are evaluated annually. The evaluation process includes the collection of student survey of instruction materials each term in each course (an evaluation form that all students complete in class about the course and the instructor's effectiveness in delivering the course content); a formal classroom visitation from the supervisor; a conference between either the dean and the adjunct instructor or the assigned full-time instructor and the adjunct instructor; and a written overall evaluation of performance. Since adjunct instructors are contracted by the term with no guarantee of future employment, it is important for the supervisor to be confident that meaningful instruction and adequate student learning be achieved in order for future contracts to be offered. In rare circumstances, the college has removed an ineffective adjunct instructor within a term and substituted another faculty member. Usually, the removed instructor is paid for the contract in full as a means to ensure contract fairness.

In addition to classroom evaluation of teaching effectiveness, other normal instructional responsibilities must be met by adjuncts: meeting all classes as assigned, and timely notification of the supervisor if emergencies prevent the adjunct from meeting class; preparation for all classes; attendance at orientation sessions; preparation and distribution of appropriate and approved syllabi; keeping informed through normal communication channels of college announcements and crucial information for students; submission of final grades in a timely manner; maintenance of class rolls; familiarity and adherence to college policies; and informing students of ways that they can contact the faculty member (telephone, email, scheduled appointments). As an added measure, the college requires all syllabi distributed by adjunct faculty to include contact information about the lead full-time instructor in the teaching discipline. All of these responsibilities are considerations used by the hiring administrator in the evaluation process and in making future contracting decisions.

Recognitions and Awards

An Excellence in Teaching Award for Adjunct Faculty is announced annually at the all-college awards program. This recognition brings with it an all-expense paid trip to the annual National Institute for Staff and Organizational Development conference, where the adjunct instructor is again recognized as outstanding. Beginning in 2000, this awardee is honored at an adjunct faculty awards reception held in conjunction with the college's fall convocation. Also honored at this celebration are the Corporate and Continuing Education Instructor of the Year and all adjunct faculty who have achieved milestones in their teaching careers at Brookhaven, beginning with those who have taught for 10 semesters. Both the longevity recognition and the excellence in teaching awards carry small mementos of the college's appreciation.

While the college has some instructors who have taught since the institution's founding in 1978, there is also a sizeable contingent who have taught between five and ten years. Brookhaven College believes that such longevity is worth recognition, and adjuncts seem to enjoy the spotlight and formal thanks from the college.

The Question of Teaching Quality

Any time a college relies on adjunct faculty for a portion of its teaching needs, it automatically comes under scrutiny by internal and external critics. That is due to an assumption that a college should provide full-time faculty members for its students—those committed individuals who not only teach but also are available for student conferences, advising, tutoring, organizational sponsorships, and the other myriad ways that faculty provide the intellectual climate necessary for a college environment. Oftentimes, accrediting agencies scrutinize colleges with large numbers of adjuncts more closely; occasionally, students question the institution that provides an adjunct instructor rather than a full-time one in front of a class.

Full-time faculty sometimes are critics of the college that uses large numbers of adjunct instructors, although that is not the situation at Brookhaven College. In many cases, full-time faculty themselves are the primary advocates for adjuncts, possibly based upon the fact that lead instructors are called upon to evaluate and mentor adjuncts and invite them to divisional meetings and to serve on college committees. At Brookhaven, full-time faculty often nominate their adjunct colleagues for faculty awards and support them during their applications for full-time employment. The college has found that engaging full-time faculty in the support of adjuncts' needs is a good way to share community with all and to improve teaching quality among the adjuncts.

In actuality, there is little evidence that adjuncts do a very different job in the classroom than do full-time instructors if student learning outcomes is the primary measure. Wyles (1998) points out that

> Evidence from my institution's experience [Northern Virginia Community College] shows that the current adjunct cohort receives student evaluations showing them to be as effective in the classroom as their full-time colleagues, that they have produced student outcomes that compete favorably with those of

full-time faculty, and that they have earned credentials of equal status to their full-time counterparts. (p. 90)

Bolge's 1995 study (as cited in McArthur, 1999) found no significant differences in the amount of learning produced in classes taught by full-time faculty and part-time faculty at Mercer County Community College. Boggs (1984) noted in his dissertation that current studies based on student evaluations had not found significant differences in the quality of instruction.

However, there is research that indicates that the fuller role of faculty members—including availability to students outside of class, participation in college governance, impact on curriculum, for instance—is missing generally from adjunct faculty expectations. Thus adjuncts are less effective in providing the full college experience for students. Based upon the 2000 Center for the Study of Community Colleges survey of 1,500 full and part-time faculty nationwide, Schuetz (2002) found that

> Although part-time faculty are generally well-qualified to perform their duties . . . it can be argued that part-timers are more weakly linked to their students, colleagues and . . . institutions than full-timers . . . less familiar with the availability of campus services [and therefore] . . . less likely to sustain extracurricular student-faculty interactions. (p. 44)

In that the literature supports the general quality of adjunct instruction but questions the fullness of the experience that adjuncts may bring to the life of the college and its students, it seems especially important for administrators to keep a close eye on the quality issue. A case in point follows.

For a college, the questions of student outcomes, faculty dependability, and curriculum continuity are issues that need constant attention. Brookhaven College implemented an initiative, called Success College, to concentrate on improvement in retention, defined simply as keeping students enrolled from the beginning of a course to the end: did they withdraw or complete? Research indicated that retention was particularly low in developmental math, an area where there were large numbers of adjunct instructors. Particularly troublesome in this discovery was the fact that the TASP laws in Texas (Texas Assessment of Student Performance) required that if a student was enrolled in remedial courses based upon TASP scores, then that student must remain enrolled in developmental/remedial course work continuously until all deficits were eliminated. If students dropped out of remedial courses (developmental math, for instance), then they must also drop out of every other course in which they were enrolled (psychology, or music, or automotive technology). Therefore, if retention in developmental math could be improved, retention college-wide would improve.

The math faculty worked to see what might be done to improve instruction and reduce the withdrawal rates in their courses. The division dean reported:

> In an attempt to improve developmental math instruction, especially from adjunct faculty, a plan was devised . . . to measure instructor effectiveness. Each instructor that taught a section of DMAT [developmental math] was measured on two variables: a) the percentage of students successfully completing the course with a C or better, and b) class median score on the standardized, departmental comprehensive final exam.

> One of the observations made from the results of the project was that, in general, full-time faculty achieved significantly higher on the two measures than the adjunct faculty. Possible explanations include that full-time faculty have a greater accessibility for students and a stronger commitment to the success of the DMAT program. (Mike Hamm, personal communication, September 15, 2003)

Upon this discovery, the college made decisions. Several more full-time developmental math instructors were hired in order to improve the full-time/adjunct ratio. Developmental math adjunct instructors were encouraged to attend the Title III workshops, previously described. Finally, based upon the discovery that exceptionally small and exceptionally large classes, regardless of the instructor, were less successful in retaining students than classes in a medium size range (25–35 students per class), class sizes were altered.

The results were rather startling. Even during a time when enrollments in developmental math were skyrocketing (average three-year growth trend per year was 10.6%), retention rates improved a full 5.5% in developmental math from 2000–2001 to 2002–2003. In addition, improvements were also noted in retention of college-level math sections by 1.5%.

The point is this: Regardless of the numbers of adjuncts a college chooses to use, it is important for the college to study the results of instruction—grade distributions, retention rates, subsequent grades made by students in sequence courses, class size as a variable—for courses taught by both full-time and part-time instructors and be willing to make changes for improvement.

Finding Adjunct Faculty

Adjunct faculty members are generally considered a group separate from the college, except for their part-time teaching responsibilities, and their connection to the college is usually looked upon as tenuous. Research studies that compare the impact of part-time faculty with full-time faculty tend to emphasize this detachment.

An adjunct instructor at Brookhaven has experienced this detachment:

> Unless I came in to the division office to turn in grades, make photo-copies, or such, I had absolutely no contact with anyone else employed here. . . . It was as if I were an arm to a body I couldn't see or feel. I had my job as an adjunct but felt no connection to anything. Students had limited access to me, and I felt uninformed when trying to answer their questions about the school.

Yet there is a sub-group of part-time faculty members who are on campus every day, all-day year round and not at all detached from the larger, ongoing life of the college. These are adjuncts that happen to be employed at the college full-time in non-teaching positions. They provide a wealth of information for students who are fortunate enough to be in their classes because they know the inner workings of the college.

One employee has been in such a role for 12 years, and his observations about his work say much about the quality and commitment of this group:

> My full-time employment as Gallery Director enables me to be readily available to students in my photography and printmaking classes, as well as to students in other classes. . . . The broad engagement with contemporary practice and theory in the visual arts that is entailed in my full-time position informs my teaching . . . and assists in helping students relate what they are learning. . . . My teaching likewise informs my gallery work.

Out of a total of 415 adjunct faculty members teaching credit courses, 35 are college employees (8%). They come from both classified and administrative positions and choose to supplement their income and fulfill their teaching interests in the same way that other adjuncts come to the college from their own work settings. Also, many of these "internal" adjuncts are employed as instructional associates, a position that involves working closely with faculty and students in lab settings. The college is fortunate to have many highly qualified and skilled laboratory-based employees. As one instructional associate said:

> Having been an IA along with the adjunct teaching in the art department for almost 5 years now, I have begun to understand the philosophy of the school, have become a part of a working team, and am certainly more aware of the operation of the department. My accessibility to students has increased along with my loyalty to the college. Now that I know the other full-time instructors in the department, we are able to share ideas on teaching, new classes, and special needs of the students. When you have an investment in something, you are willing to give more of yourself. With that in mind, I now feel as if I 'represent' Brookhaven as opposed to just teaching here as an adjunct.

Adjunct Service and Full-Time Teaching Options

Many adjuncts assume that their prospects for full-time employment at the college of their choice are dim. Of course, many adjuncts are not interested in becoming college faculty full-time. They teach as an outlet, for the supplementary income, or for other reasons. However, a good number of them would like nothing better than to be able to move into the ranks of the full-time faculty in a setting that is familiar. In preparation for this chapter, the authors questioned Brookhaven's deans about the number of current full-time faculty in their divisions who were previously adjuncts, either at Brookhaven College or at some other institution. In fine arts/physical education, 15 out of the 19 current full-time faculty had taught part-time. In the communications/social science division, 9 out of 15 full-time faculty came from the ranks of adjuncts. And in math/science, almost half (44%) started as adjunct faculty.

For Brookhaven, it seems that teaching somewhere as a part-time faculty member is a definite plus for moving into the full-time ranks. It would also appear that with the leading edge of faculty retirements upon community colleges, the prospects for excellent adjunct faculty to make up the core of a new generation of full-time faculty are bright.

Adjunct Faculty Teaching Corporate and Continuing Education Courses

This chapter would not be complete without information about Brookhaven's part-time instructors in the Division of Corporate and Continuing Education. CCE instructors must demonstrate expertise appropriate to their individual fields, but since programs in CCE are geared toward workforce education, they are not subject to the same credentials required for credit transfer faculty by regional and state accreditation agencies. Yet in many cases their experience is extraordinary: CCE instructor ranks at Brookhaven have included an advisor to the State Department and the curator of the Alamo. They may be gainfully employed in business and industry or retirees, but they enjoy sharing their professional expertise through teaching.

Recruitment of these instructors is primarily through job fairs, referrals from other colleges, or business and industry. Contracts are generated by our district with standard clauses. However, if a class does not attain the required minimum number of registered students, an instructor can renegotiate the pay rate so that the class can still be offered. Since pay is market driven, it ranges from as low as $5 (this low rate meeting the income criteria for some retirees, not because of the college's stinginess!) to as much as $80 per hour for highly technical programs. The average pay is $24 per hour. Evaluation of CCE instructors is overseen by college program managers with student evaluations taken in every class.

"We couldn't run CCE without adjuncts. It wouldn't exist. They generate the local revenue source because they are almost all part-time," explains the Executive Dean of Corporate and Continuing Education. "They are typically highly qualified."

Summary and Conclusions

Brookhaven College would not be what it is without adjunct faculty: They are essential to the fullness of students' academic experience because they allow the college to provide quality education on a wider scale and in greater depth than would otherwise be possible. Indeed, as citizen-educators, they provide students something no one else at the college really can: an example of serving others for the sake of education, the love of learning, and the good of the community.

Note

The authors wish to thank their colleagues for their assistance: Ray Attner, Rodger Bennett, Ann Coder, Resi Douglas, Juanita Flint, Mike Hamm, Barbara Lattanzio, Nancy LeCroy, Linda Lee, Cindi Love, Marilyn Kolesar Lynch, Zack Miller, Susan Mollet, David Newman, Susan Osgood, Carrie Schweitzer, Teri Walker, and Sheila Williams.

References

Boggs, G. R. (1984). *An evaluation of the instructional effectiveness of part-time community college developmental writing faculty.* Unpublished doctoral dissertation, University of Texas at Austin. (ERIC Document Reproduction Service No. ED463038)

McArthur, R. C. (1999). A comparison of grading patterns between full- and part-time humanities faculty: A preliminary study. *Community College Review, 27*(3), 65.

Priest, B. (1967). *Report of the chancellor.* Unpublished annual report presented to the Dallas County Community College District.

Schuetz, P. (2002). Instructional practices of part-time and full-time faculty. In C. L. Outcalt (Ed.), *New directions for community colleges: No. 118. Community college faculty: Characteristics, practices, and challenges* (pp. 39–46). San Francisco, CA: Jossey-Bass.

Wyles, B. (1998). Adjunct faculty in the community college: Realities and challenges. In D. W. Leslie (Ed.), *New directions for higher education: No. 104. The growing use of part-time faculty: Understanding causes and effects* (pp. 89–93). San Francisco, CA: Jossey-Bass.

7 | RETENTION OF PART-TIME FACULTY

Helen Burnstad and Joseph L. Gadberry

Gappa and Leslie (1993) caught the attention of postsecondary education institutions with their book, *The Invisible Faculty*. With their publication came the hope that adjunct faculty might begin to receive the attention and resources they need and deserve. Roueche, Roueche, and Milliron (1995) published their study, *Strangers in Their Own Land*, identifying the lack of inclusion, resources, and respect generally granted to part-time faculty in community colleges. Today, Alfred (2003) continues the cry for better attention to be paid to adjunct faculty.

> Adjunct faculty are the largest payroll group in our colleges by headcount and our reliance upon them is increasing. Yet, we pay them poorly, provide them with marginal support, and barely connect them to the institution. Office space and a computer are a luxury, as are most other basic amenities. We do not effectively orient part-timers to our core values, invest in their development, or evaluate their performance. For a group that is a primary point of contact with the institution for many students, how can we place so much trust in their work and provide such a shabby response to their needs? We are expecting a lot from people we are unwilling to invest in. (p. 20)

This is a dismal situation when our colleges rely on adjunct faculty to teach over 40% of all courses (Wickun & Stanley, 2000).

The research on part-time faculty documents that "part-timers have strong feelings about whether they are or are not 'connected' to or 'integrated' into campus life. For the most part, they feel powerless, alienated, invisible, and second class" (Gappa & Leslie, 1993, p. 180). As colleges continue to hire an increasingly larger number of adjunct faculty (Cox, 2000; Leatherman, 2000), due in part to fiscal constraints and enrollment pressures, administrators must seek ways of connecting and including these faculty to our institutions. Integration into our institutions will be a way of ensuring that " . . . part-time faculty members are successful, valued, and supported in what they do" (Gappa & Leslie, 1993, p. 180).

This chapter will overview a number of strategies that have been successfully employed to create an institutional climate of inclusion. The strategies will be developed in terms of welcoming adjuncts to the college, providing infrastructure support, giving the adjunct faculty a voice on the campus, preparing them to be effective instructors, and celebrating their contributions to the college and to student success.

Inclusion promotes retention of part-time faculty. Retention is vital because of the cost of recruiting new adjunct faculty, as well as the cost to the college when it has to cancel classes if qualified adjunct instructors are not available. Another potential cost is the burnout of full-time faculty if they are encouraged to teach overload when part-timers cannot be found. Full-timers will take on the overload because of their strong motivation to serve students. Retention of adjunct faculty is in the best interest of the college.

Welcoming Adjunct Faculty to the College

From their very first contact with the college, all efforts should reflect a professionalism that is supportive of the need for part-time faculty as well as a welcoming encouragement of them. The position description, posting, and advertising from the human resources office should all be professional and communicate the clear message that adjunct faculty are a valued resource of the instructional staff of the college. A systematic means of providing information should be developed to assist those interested in seeking part-time faculty positions. College/department adjunct faculty checklists, frequently asked questions (FAQs), email contacts, even a web site devoted to adjunct faculty issues are all helpful resources for providing information to potential adjunct faculty.

As outlined in Chapter 5, careful attention needs to be given to the posting, screening, interviewing, and orienting process. Information on teaching requirements, rights and responsibilities of adjunct faculty, benefits, and professional development opportunities are critical during the hiring and orientation process. It is especially helpful to provide information on the student population to adjunct faculty as they express interest in a position. It may come as a big surprise that they will have a class where the age range may be from 15 years old to 85 years old or they may anticipate a classroom just of returning adults only to find one filled with traditional aged students of 17–22. Adjunct faculty will appreciate information about the classroom, the students, and the teaching expectations.

From posting a position through the hiring interview, colleges need to adopt an inviting and welcoming attitude toward part-time faculty. These early encounters with the department/division chair, human resources department, and full-time faculty will establish a mental model and perception of the college culture while simultaneously communicating an attitude of value and inclusion for adjunct faculty. Welcoming, hiring, and orientation strategies include and integrate part-time faculty into the college.

Providing Infrastructure Support for Adjunct Faculty

Welcoming part-time faculty to campus is important. Retaining them after successful hiring and orientation is critical. Experts agree that replacing a talented employee costs at least two-and-a-half times his or her annual salary. In addition to this cost colleges must factor in the resources of time and energy devoted to hiring and orientating by department/division chairs, human resource officers, and full-time faculty serving on adjunct hiring committees.

Providing infrastructure support for part-time faculty includes a college's commitment to providing space, support services, communication means, and supplies for adjunct faculty. Consider the following examples of infrastructure support as they contribute to retention of part-time faculty: office space; storage space; conference space, or at least a private meeting room where they can confer with students; clerical support—typing and printing services; sample materials including sample syllabus for the class assigned, sample handouts, exams, supplemental texts; resources about teaching and learning; mailbox; email address; voice mail system access; Center for Teaching and Learning (CTL); instructional support; training on the use of technology. This is just a partial list of the kinds of infrastructure support and resources a college can provide to adjunct faculty. In the end, the more at home adjunct faculty feel, the more likely they are to be successful and continue as a valuable resource for the college.

Giving Adjunct Faculty a Voice on the Campus

Part-time faculty need to have a voice on campus. This can be accomplished by a number of strategies. In some schools part-time faculty have an association that provides a method of meeting and supporting the needs of part-time faculty. In other institutions, part-time faculty are given a voice through membership in the same faculty senate or professional organization as full-time faculty. And in other colleges and states, part-time faculty have felt the need to unionize to have a voice.

If the college does not currently have a formal method for hearing the voice of part-time faculty, the chief academic officer may invite departments to select a part-time faculty member to serve on an advisory council that meets as needed with the academic leader. This method also can become a means of getting support for projects that will enrich the life of part-time faculty. The opportunity to contribute by having their voice heard on campus will go a long way toward integrating part-time faculty into the campus culture. Once integrated, part-time faculty are more likely to want to continue to contribute to the instructional mission of the college.

Preparing Part-Time Faculty to Be Effective Instructors

The importance of adjunct faculty roles as effective teachers should be emphasized from the posting of the position, through the interview, into the orientation material both print and personal, by the mentor assigned to him or her, and as supported by the immediate academic supervisor.

The position description for part-time faculty should be stressed during the interview. The description includes statements of behaviors that ensure effective instruction such as preparation of appropriate course materials, including the course syllabus and final assessment methods.

Materials provided during the orientation can include resources about effective teaching such as *A Handbook for Adjunct/Part-Time Faculty and Teachers of Adults* by Donald Greive (2003), guest speakers, teaching tips brochures, and simple teaching strategies printed on cards or book marks. Including teaching and learning resources with the orientation materials communicates to adjunct faculty that effective teaching strategies are important. It becomes clear that the college expects outstanding teaching and is willing to invest resources to help the adjunct faculty be successful.

A part-time mentor system is an excellent way to provide support as well as training. Some programs will assign either a full-time faculty member to each part-timer or an effective adjunct. The mentor plan provides for some other link besides the program leader or support person to connect the college to the part-timer, thus helping to reduce the feeling of isolation. Mentors are trained to be supportive and to help guarantee effective student learning. Their role may be focused on the curriculum or it may be focused on the transition to the college. No one model works equally well in all organizations.

At Johnson County Community College (JCCC), as with many community colleges, part-time faculty are encouraged to use the resources in the CTL. The center sponsors workshop, institutes, and discussion opportunities to pursue effectiveness in the classroom. The center has print, electronic, media, and human resources to help adjunct faculty prepare for class, use innovative teaching and learning strategies, learn and understand a wide range of instructional pedagogies, prepare for the demands of assessing student learning outcomes, and stay current in their discipline.

One of the ways that JCCC uses the CTL to advance the teaching effectiveness of part-time faculty is to provide Adjunct Certification Training (ACT). The ACT program is a program designed to benefit the students, adjunct faculty, and JCCC as an institution in general.

Adjunct Certification Training Program

Part-time faculty apply to participate in the ACT program through a letter of support from the assistant dean and a statement of intended learning outcomes. The application also requires a current resume. The goal of ACT is to provide tools and resources that assist adjunct faculty in becoming more effective educators in the classroom. Certification requires an adjunct faculty member to complete seven specifically noted modules and at least one optional module. These are to be completed within a two-semester sequence with the option to extend for one additional year. Upon completion of ACT, the adjunct instructor should be:

1) Cognizant of the college's mission
2) Aware of policies and procedures of the academic branch
3) Comfortable in the college's learning community
4) Equipped with more resources to enhance student learning in the classroom

ACT is limited to 40 participants each year. All adjunct faculty members are encouraged to apply for ACT. Primary consideration is given to adjunct faculty who have an individual development plan on file in the Office of Staff and Organizational Development, the recommendation of the assistant dean, and limited or no teaching experience.

The ACT program consists of eight modules.

1) **Orientation and narrative reflections.** This module is an overview of the program, including strategies for becoming a

reflective practitioner. The product of the ACT program becomes a reflective journal which must be completed and submitted before an ACT certificate is conferred.

2) **Employment policies and procedures.** This module examines the policies and procedures of the college. The record keeping forms needed to complete the work of an instructor are provided and discussed.

3) **Technology.** This module outlines the use of Misty City Gradebook and Pipeline. Effective use of the campus Banner System provides adjunct faculty important electronic systems for contacting students.

4) **Designing effective instruction.** This module focuses on preparing an effective syllabus. Careful attention to standards, outcomes, class requirements, assignments, and so on are discussed during this module. Adjunct faculty learn the power and importance of designing an effective syllabus as a critical tool for instruction, communication, and assessment.

5) **Challenges of students.** This module describes the students at JCCC and analyzes the impact of student demographics on the classroom. Knowing the audience provides important information on how to design instruction, expectations, and learning outcomes.

6) **Legal issues/diversity.** This module explains legal issues in a postsecondary setting. Issues regarding harassment and discrimination are discussed, and clear expectations of equality and professional behavior are communicated.

7) **Enhancing effective instruction.** In this module adjunct faculty discover how to design lessons that are easy to construct, clear, and simple for students to follow. Adjunct faculty bring their syllabus, course outline and outcomes, and a unit of instruction to work on.

8) **Microteaching session/videotaping of classroom activity.** This module includes the opportunity for adjunct faculty to be videotaped in their classroom. In addition, adjunct faculty have the opportunity to receive feedback and coaching with a trained ACT facilitator after the videotaping session.

In addition to these eight modules, adjunct faculty may select one of the following electives.

1) **Effective Communication and Listening Skills: Did You Hear What I Thought I Said?** This module provides adjunct faculty with an opportunity to interact with other professionals as they learn the dynamics of effective listening and communication.

2) **Basic Principles for a Collaborative Workplace.** This module is an overview session providing a foundation for interaction in the JCCC learning community. The five basic principles serve as guidelines for behavior that put the organization's shared values into practice while developing a strong network of productive relationships at every level of the organization.

3) **Teaching Techniques: Beyond the Lecture.** This module includes a sampling of teaching techniques beyond the normal lecture approach. Classroom feedback strategies are also included.

4) **Test Construction—Wear Your Hard Hat: Test Under Construction.** Adjunct faculty will identify a variety of ways to evaluate progress and learning outcomes in the classroom during this module.

5) **Learning Styles: What a Brain!** This module examines a variety of learning style instruments and their use in the classroom.

6) **Understanding Yourself and Others: Who Are You?** This module helps adjunct faculty understand their work behavioral styles using a Personal Profile System. Work styles are discussed in relation to teaching and learning to enhance faculty effectiveness in the classroom.

A final outcome of the program is the development of the Individual Development Plan, which assists part-time faculty members in career advancement. After completing the modules and submitting the reflective journal, the part-time faculty member receives a one-time stipend of $800. Faculty are also presented a certificate of completion and a book on teaching and learning at the faculty awards dinner held each spring to celebrate adjunct faculty.

Other Resources for Retention

JCCC uses the ACT program to integrate, inculcate, and retain adjunct faculty. Other community colleges use a wide range of similar strategies to integrate and include part-timers. Some schools are using the Learning Exchange Network materials prepared by the League for Innovation in Community Colleges. This material is well designed and can be used as a self-study course or during face-to-face workshops.

Online training for adjunct faculty is being developed by a number of schools. Valencia Community College, Indian River Community College, 4faculty.org, and other programs are actively being developed and distributed.

College Center for Teaching and Learning

A college center for teaching and learning provides another opportunity to retain adjunct faculty. The CTL is a faculty-based program counseled by a campus-wide advisory committee. One of the guiding principles of the CTL is "by faculty, for faculty." JCCC faculty members take ownership in the CTL by establishing initiatives and by leading their colleagues through these initiatives. The CTL seeks to enhance teaching and learning, improve student and faculty success, and stimulate educational effectiveness. The CTL integrates and includes part-time faculty within the membership of the Center Resource Team and as participants in all center activities. The center provides individual consultation in numerous educational specialties, hosts a variety of faculty (full- and part-time) workshops and seminars, and offers a wide range of instructional resources.

The CTL has physical space on campus; however, programs and resources can be delivered where faculty members need them. The CTL houses a library with teaching and learning resources for all faculty to use, a space for faculty to meet with colleagues or connect with a group to talk about teaching and learning. The CTL gives full- and part-time faculty voice and ownership. Each department/program area appoints a faculty liaison who works directly with CTL in planning and promoting faculty development activities that address needs and interests across departments/programs—full- and part-time, senior and junior, credit and non-credit, vocational and liberal arts. The CTL provides programming and services of its own and helps faculty connect with all existing campus resources. The CTL's program of instructional innovation and improvement supports the diverse needs of the JCCC educational community and the college's stated mission. The CTL is an essential component of JCCC retention efforts for part-time faculty.

Master Teachers Workshop

One of the most beneficial retention strategies for continuing adjunct faculty is the Master Teachers Workshop (MTW). JCCC's in-house MTW is held during January in-service. For the past 13 years, many faculty members—full- and part-time—have taken part in this exciting opportunity and unique format. Faculty reaction has been consistently supportive and outstandingly positive as they return to their classes revitalized and energized with new strategies for delivering course content. Thirty-five JCCC faculty members, representing a cross section of the college's diverse full- and part-time faculty participate in the three-day event. A residential setting is chosen for the MTW. The workshop is designed to promote collegiality through sharing ideas, successes, and concerns related to teaching and learning. The MTW is designed and facilitated entirely by JCCC full- and part-time faculty who have participated in the workshop, shadowed facilitators in a mentoring role, and co-facilitated with colleagues from the college. In this way, the faculty totally own the process of MTW at JCCC. The goals of the workshop are to celebrate the activities of teaching and to seek solutions to issues faced by teachers.

At JCCC, part-time faculty are included in all in-service programs as well as the MTW. These in-service programs and the MTW provide opportunities for full-time and adjunct faculty to explore effective strategies as well as to seek support from each other on how to deal with issues of concern in the classroom. In-service workshops and the MTW provide critical opportunities for adjunct faculty to feel valued and included in important issues related to teaching and learning.

Adjunct Semester Refresher

The Adjunct Semester Refresher grew out of a JCCC Office of Institutional Research study completed in 2000. Of the 305 adjuncts that completed the JCCC Adjunct Faculty Survey almost all indicated that some type of refresher orientation should be held for adjuncts who have taught at the college for several semesters. The Adjunct Semester Refresher was initiated in the spring of 2002. The refreshers are held one evening during the fall or spring semester in-service.

Adjunct instructors who have taught at the college for seven or more semesters receive an invitation to participate. The invitation is sent out approximately four weeks prior to the event. Adjuncts must return an RSVP to facilitate planning for the dinner and supplies for the workshop. Three separate professional development opportunities are offered concurrently and facilitated by JCCC faculty members. The facilitators are current and/or former associates of the CTL. The evening begins with a greeting by the vice president for instruction and a dinner. A JCCC video, *It's Where You Belong,* that highlights the college and the students is shown.

There are three separate one-hour concurrent sessions offered twice during the evening, and the adjuncts must indicate at the time of registration which two sessions they want to attend. Topics for sessions have included classroom assessment, student learning styles, tips for teaching a three-hour class, service learning, learning communities, relating brain research and classroom practices, technology use in the classroom, engaging the student learner, and test construction.

At the conclusion of the Adjunct Semester Refresher, each participant is given materials, including a tote bag with the college logo and the event name. Faculty response to the Semester Refresher has been very good, it is a way to give adjunct faculty who may have previously felt excluded on the JCCC campus an opportunity to develop continuing relationships with new full- and part-time faculty.

Celebrating the Contributions of Adjunct Faculty

Celebrating the contributions of adjunct faculty to the college and to student success builds community among adjunct faculty and among all members of the campus community. Kouzes and Posner (2002) encourage organizations to build community by celebrating values and victories together. Celebrating community reinforces the fact that extraordinary performance is the result of many people's efforts. The college's success is built upon the extraordinary performance of many people, including adjunct faculty. If 50% of the instructional staff are adjunct faculty, clearly student success is the result of the extraordinary performance of adjunct faculty.

When adjunct faculty are hired for excellence, oriented into the campus culture, integrated and retained as valued members of the instructional staff, extraordinary performance occurs. "By celebrating people's accomplishments visibly and in group settings leaders create and sustain team spirit; by basing celebrations on the accomplishment of key values and milestones, they sustain people's focus" (Kouzes & Posner, 2002, p. 368).

Featuring part-time faculty in internal publications is one way of recognizing their contribution to the college. Part-time faculty should be invited to share teaching successes in internal newsletters. Many community college publications, such as *The Community College Times* and the Chair Academy's *Academic Leadership* journal, are interested in news and articles on or by part-time faculty.

Special awards are often established for teaching excellence for part-time faculty members. These awards define the college's expectations of excellent teaching and provide important recognition to part-time faculty for the valued contribution they make to excellence and teaching and learning.

JCCC received a generous donation for adjunct faculty teaching excellence recognition in 1997–1998. This gift is used to honor adjunct faculty during a dinner each spring. The dinner is the culmination of an award process where part-time faculty from each department/division are recognized and honored. Each nominee receives a plaque and six are chosen from the pool to receive monetary awards.

In addition, adjunct faculty members completing the ACT program are recognized for their achievement.

Summary and Conclusions

Retaining effective part-time faculty is in the best interest of full-time faculty, administrators, and students. When adjunct faculty are welcomed to campus, provided infrastructure support for their success, have the opportunity to design and deliver professional development initiatives that broaden and deepen their knowledge and skills in teaching and learning, and recognize and celebrate their achievements, they feel successful, valued, and supported.

References

Alfred, R. (2003). The wolf at the door. *Community College Journal, 73*(5), 16–24.

Cox, A. M. (2000, December 1). Study shows colleges' dependence on their part-time instructors: Report documents the low pay and lack of benefits for those off the tenure track. *Chronicle of Higher Education,* p. A12.

Gappa, J. M., & Leslie, D. W. (1993). *The invisible faculty: Improving the status of part-timers in higher education.* San Francisco, CA: Jossey-Bass.

Greive, D. (2003). *A handbook for adjunct/part-time faculty and teachers of adults* (4th ed.). Ann Arbor, MI: Adjunct Advocate.

Kouzes, J. M., & Posner, B. Z. (2002). *The leadership challenge: How to keep getting extraordinary things done in organizations.* San Francisco, CA: Jossey-Bass.

Leatherman, C. (2000, January 28). Part-timers continue to replace full-timers on college faculties: Education department report says adjuncts now make up nearly half the professoriate. *Chronicle of Higher Education,* p. A18.

Roueche, J. E., Roueche, S. D., & Milliron, M. D. (1995). *Strangers in their own land: Part-time faculty in American community colleges.* Washington, DC: Community College Press.

Wickun, W. G., & Stanley, R. F. (2003). *The role of adjunct faculty in higher education.* Retrieved October 14, 2003, from http://mtprof.msun.edu/Win2000/Wickun.html

8 | A STRATEGIC MODEL FOR INTEGRATING PREPARED ADJUNCT FACULTY INTO THE COLLEGE CULTURE

Richard E. Lyons

During the fall of 1994, a group of department chairs and instructional administrators at Indian River Community College (IRCC) began what would become an extended conversation about their adjunct faculty. Grounded in the quality management movement, several were concerned about the impact of part-time instructors who were poorly prepared to manage their initial teaching assignments. Several others were frustrated by gaps in communication with potential and already employed adjunct instructors, which had fostered critical problems that they viewed as preventable. All had been embarrassed by incidents that had harmed several key adjunct instructors, whom they viewed as essential to the success of their instructional units. With the understanding and support of the college president, this initially small group of instructional leaders launched what they knew would be an extended process to maximize the quality of instruction delivered by adjunct faculty members of the five-campus, rapidly growing college, and to foster a collegial culture of teaching excellence that would fully include part-timers in the pursuit of the college's mission. In an August 2003 comprehensive survey of the college's adjunct faculty members, the effort demonstrated its effectiveness, when nearly 70% reported feeling "like a true member of the IRCC faculty." The strategic plan, its tactical action steps, and the evaluative information that drove and explained this transformation are the focus of this chapter.

Establishing the Foundation

Through recent graduate coursework, academic conference sessions and professional reading, participants in the early discussion had learned of the relatively quiet but growing nationwide dialogue on adjunct faculty issues. Although limited in sound research, the conventional wisdom of the day seemed to be that the proportion of courses taught by adjunct faculty at most institutions was growing extensively, that as full-timers retired their teaching loads were being supplanted by assignments to part-time instructors, and that the trend toward increased usage of adjunct faculty was being viewed as permanent. The anecdotal evidence of increasing numbers of "freeway flyers" and "roads scholars" who taught concurrently for several institutions was gaining widespread exposure and driving perceptions of the growth of an academic underclass. As their discussions became more frequent and intense, the group's members decided that action must be taken to ensure that this apparent trend did not create problems with the teaching culture of the college that would be much more difficult to manage if they delayed to act.

The group's first formal step was to establish a standing faculty committee that included several key instructional deans as ex officio members. When informed and constructive individuals heard of the effort, recruiting committee members in addition to the core group of discussants was an especially easy task and provided broader representation of instructional units and diversity of viewpoints. All members of the new committee embraced the compelling mission of the committee's work fully. The committee's first meeting brought many concerns and anecdotes to the surface that deserved consideration. However, recognizing the potential of reacting to "the squeakiest wheel" syndrome, several leaders lobbied for a research-driven approach that would identify the issues whose solution would have the greatest impact on the long-term effectiveness of the committee's work. That approach won support easily and became a driving force throughout the history of the committee. To that end, it was decided at the first meeting to launch the committee's work with an intensive survey of the college's existing adjunct faculty members.

Shortly thereafter, one of the committee's members obtained a copy of Gappa and Leslie's *The Invisible Faculty* (1993), which had begun to make higher education leaders more aware of the dimensions of the part-time faculty situation throughout North America. That member read it thoroughly and then circulated it throughout the committee's other members. Each discovered—in a darkly comforting way—that a neglectful posture toward adjunct instructors permeated most institutions of higher education in North America—universities and liberal arts colleges, as well as community colleges. However, they also read that among the array of institutional types studied, Gappa and Leslie had found that community colleges employed by far the greatest aggregate number and percentage of part-time faculty. Committee members concluded that it was even more critical than for those in other institutional types to address the issue boldly and in a spirit of collegiality. Although its ratio of full- to part-time faculty members was found not to mirror that of the community colleges studied, no committee member found solace in being "no worse than anyone else." Instead they embraced fully the call to arms of Gappa and Leslie:

> It is time to admit (because of budgetary and planning realities) that part-timers are a substantial and permanent part of the academic profession and should be treated as such. We do not foresee any real aggregate diminution in their use, and we advocate the adoption of fair and equitable policies that will help them play constructive roles in providing quality education. (p. 91)

Research and Assessment

As a subcommittee was appointed to begin developing a survey of the needs and perceptions of the college's adjunct faculty members, a second national study, with an equally ominous title, was published. For those in community and technical colleges however, the message of *Strangers in Their Own Land* (Roueche, Roueche, & Milliron, 1995) was even more compelling than that of *The Invisible Faculty* because it focused solely on practices toward part-time faculty members within two-year institutions. Its findings confirmed many of those in *The*

Invisible Faculty that little or no difference could be found between the teaching abilities of full- and part-time faculty, and that often part-timers were, on average, held to a higher standard of teaching performance than their full-time colleagues. These findings brought to bear the importance of developing a comprehensive set of strategies that supported and helped retain this increasingly critical part-time human resource.

The newly-organized adjunct faculty committee leveraged the findings of *The Invisible Faculty* and *Strangers in Their Own Land* studies, the results of its own initial needs survey, and those of several focus group meetings to develop a grounded understanding of the college's diverse adjunct faculty members. Among the findings that dovetailed with the national studies were that IRCC's adjunct faculty—nearly evenly divided between those teaching academic transfer courses, occupational courses, and adult education programs such as GED and ESL—was comprised nearly totally of the two profiles Gappa and Leslie (1993) identified as *specialist, expert or professionals,* and *career enders.* It included very few *aspiring academics* of which so much had been written and was driving perceptions nationwide, or *freelancers*— individuals who by choice pursue several part-time jobs that include a regular college teaching assignment. These findings made sense given the fact that IRCC's four-county service district includes a significant population of upscale retirees and is not home to the primary campus of a major research university.

Findings and Application

The critical design features of the committee's strategic plan were largely the product of its own primary research. Among their findings were a widespread perception among its adjunct faculty members of ineffective access to and communications with their instructional leaders and a sense of isolation that those engender; inconvenient and insufficient support services; lack of a base of technical skills in teaching and classroom management; and inequity in pay with full-timers. While bad news is seldom welcome, the findings were not surprising nor inconsistent with the national studies. Realizing the limits of college resources, the committee members were adamant about initiating effective responses without raising expectations that might not be sustainable. They first focused their energies on improving communications because genuine improvements could be demonstrated rather immediately, and were affordable.

Improved communications tactics that were initiated included a major overhaul of the annual meeting that all adjunct instructors were required to attend, a major revision of the adjunct faculty handbook distributed annually and heretofore reviewed at that meeting, and the publication and widespread distribution of a quarterly newsletter. The planning and delivery of the annual meeting was assigned to an enthusiastic, positive administrator and its format transformed from a review of the handbook into a professional development activity. Institutional change plans became the focus of a highly visual presentation delivered by the college president, with an eye toward diminishing adjuncts' sense of isolation and fostering instead one of inclusion and collegiality. The handbook was made more reader-friendly through more effective layout and the addition of graphics. Each issue of the newsletter addressed a half dozen frequently asked questions about college policies and procedures, a detailed teaching or classroom management tip, and the profile of a successful part-time instructor that was rotated among instructional areas to foster widespread interest. With the installation of these measures, the members of the committee and stakeholders in their success sensed that their work was getting traction.

As would be seen in other components later, the communications strategies were evaluated continuously and refined frequently to make them more valuable to adjunct instructors. For example, in 2002 each adjunct faculty member was provided a college email account to facilitate interactions with members of the adjunct faculty committee, their department chairs and other instructional leaders, and their students. Efforts were made to provide adjunct instructors with access to a wide range of information that flowed through the email system to encourage them to begin using their IRCC account regularly. Each monthly issue of the human resources department's online newsletter designed originally for full-time faculty, staff, and administrators, which had been launched the previous year, was customized for adjunct faculty members and distributed through a hyperlink in an email message delivered via an adjunct distribution list.

Dedicated to basing its strategies and tactics on sound data, the committee increased the quality and the quantity of its future information base by leveraging the college's staff and professional development budget and liberal sabbatical policy. While pursuing my doctoral degree, I focused my dissertation research on the professional development of adjunct faculty. My qualitative study employed face-to-face mentoring interviews with and the journal writings of 22 adjunct instructors from across the spectrum of disciplines. It also employed focus groups of additional adjunct instructors and interviews with instructional leaders to delve more deeply into the part-time teaching environment. The study found, among other things, that participants required a grounded foundation of teaching and classroom management skills, a more thorough orientation to the institution and their teaching assignments, social learning opportunities, and more accessible professional development resources. It concluded by recommending the implementation of a program to address these needs (Lyons, 1996).

The Adjunct Faculty Development Initiative

In the fall of 1996, these recommendations were addressed by the launch of a comprehensive initiative for all of the adjunct instructors within one of the college's larger instructional divisions. Its components included:

- A thorough orientation by the department chair or his or her designee that employed a newly developed checklist to address the full array of issues that influence the success of an adjunct instructor's teaching
- A course titled "Instructor Effectiveness Training" (see Appendix 8A for the course syllabus), required for all new adjunct instructors prior to or concurrent with their initial teaching assignment, which would focus on teaching and classroom management basics
- A mentoring program between each new adjunct instructor and a veteran full- or part-time instructor, designed to fill in the gaps

of the course's curriculum and make applications to the instructor's specific course

- A series of meal meetings to remedy the widespread isolation perceived by adjuncts reported in the national studies, at which new and veteran, full- and part-time faculty members could socialize and participate in a professional development opportunity
- A materials resource center that contained donated books and papers on key topics areas and was designed for use by all instructors, but with special invitations being regularly communicated to adjunct faculty members

Adjunct instructors often report that their initial teaching assignment meeting sounded something like, "The class starts this Tuesday night. Here is a copy of the textbook and a syllabus from last semester. Call if you need help." Such orientations to part-time teaching are unfortunately all too common—and often set the adjunct instructor up for failure to achieve the level of success that is expected in the increasingly accountable environment of community college education. In planning a more effective, manageable orientation regimen, committee members and instructional deans invested several hours in developing a checklist that addressed the array of issues affecting part-time instructors that has been increasingly employed by department chairs to guide their individual or small-group sessions. Over 83% of the respondents in the 2003 survey, which included those who began teaching prior to the implementation of the initiative, reported having received an orientation, and 86% of these said that it was well managed.

Instructor Effectiveness Course

From the launch of the initiative, its cornerstone was the Instructor Effectiveness Training course. Beginning a week or two before each fall and spring semester, the course's sessions focus on course planning, managing the course effectively, effective teaching and learning methods, and evaluating student achievement and teaching effectiveness. Besides the achievement of those objectives, the 200 adjunct faculty members and 30 full-timers who have completed it have also fostered collegial relationships and identified valuable teaching resources that would have otherwise not been discovered. As instructional deans and department chairs have received feedback on its success, the number of discipline areas represented by participants has steadily increased.

In addition to the information that the course imparts, the course has provided an opportunity to evaluate the critical thinking skills and attitudes of new instructors, thus enabling more effective course assignments. Its journaling assignment provides practice in analyzing teaching and learning situations and grounds participants' understanding in sound theory and best practices. Lastly, while difficult to quantify, the course has unquestionably affected the retention of students enrolled in the participants' course sections, as well as the retention of the instructors themselves. In spite of the fact that the course is scheduled on four Saturday mornings, its textbook must be purchased by the participant, and no additional remuneration is provided for the time in class, 74% of the survey respondents completing the course, indicated that it prepared them well to be a successful instructor.

Early in 2002, the course was adapted into three online versions for delivery to an increasingly time-challenged body of adjunct instructors. One version focused on the needs of those who teach academic transfer courses, another on the needs of those delivering occupational courses, and the third for instructors who teach adult education programs. Launched in the fall 2002 term, the online courses enable acceleration of completion, provide time and place convenience over the traditional classroom-based course, and focus instructional content more tightly on the discipline area of the participant. For example, the adult education version, which targets those who teach GED and ESL courses, emphasizes mastery of the one-on-one strategies more common in that teaching environment. The success of the classroom-based course had generated the publication of a textbook (Lyons, Kysilka, & Pawlas, 1999) that the instructors and participants in the online course found very effective. The downside of the online version includes greater attrition and a limited ability to contribute to the building of a community of learners within the college overall. Only 51% of the respondents who had completed the online version reported that it prepared them well to be an effective instructor. Thus, the classroom-based version that delivers a significantly higher level of effectiveness for those who prefer the face-to-face contact and spontaneity it provides will be continued.

Mentoring

Designed to provide completers of the course with support in applying its content and to reduce the sense of isolation that adjunct instructors commonly experience, the mentoring component was structured to provide maximum flexibility. Unlike programs at other institutions where new instructors are assigned mentors based upon arbitrary factors considered significant by a program coordinator, the IRCC approach provided mentors and their mentees several planned opportunities to meet in groups, and encouraged their voluntary selection of a partner with whom they could forge a mutually beneficial mentoring relationship. A number of mentoring relationships were initiated by new and veteran instructors who taught in adjoining classrooms, new instructors who were recruited to teaching by a veteran instructor with whom they shared an employer, membership in a civic or religious organization, and similar situations. Teaching is a field that has demonstrated a natural and historical culture of mentoring, and it seems to thrive on synergistic opportunities. So as adjuncts discovered that others were engaged in mentoring relationships, it became a model for others to emulate. The August 2003 study found that 67% of respondents had been mentored by at least one person at IRCC, and of these, 82% found the experience effective.

Social Activities and Recognition

Beginning with the launch of the initiative in 1996, two social events have had a positive impact on the success of the entire effort. The first has been a series of brown-bag luncheons. The agendas are evenly divided between sharing a meal and a professional development activity for all faculty members within the instructional unit. Initially scheduled for the first Friday in each month, the first occurred in the fall semester's early weeks and fostered the greatest attendance of all that would follow. Its professional development activity was focused on the benefits of mentoring relationships and delivered by the instructional dean, which no doubt contributed to the early success of that component. Subsequent presentations focused on the use of cooperative learning and the implementation of electronic grade books, and an end-of-the-academic year session that provided attendees the opportunity to share their richest teaching experiences. Besides the introductions to a wide range of colleagues and the information sharing that the brown-bag luncheons engendered, they also provided time for individuals to share teaching strategies and materials and an environment in which deeper relationships have been fostered.

The initial brown-bag luncheon series also provided other instructional divisions and departments a model upon which to craft their own version of the activity—some of which have been conducted in the morning or late afternoon, and a few on Saturday morning. Each unit has achieved similar outcomes, that is, more effectively equipped faculty members who felt better connected to their colleagues. Although schedule conflicts and driving distance prevent these types of activities from achieving an ideal attendance—only 38% of respondents in the adjunct survey reported having participated—they nonetheless nurture a culture of learning that would not otherwise have been possible.

The second social event that was initiated in the 1996 plan was an annual end-of-year, off-campus wine and cheese party that celebrates the contributions of the college's adjunct faculty members. Cosponsored by the college's chapter of the Florida Association of Community Colleges, the event provides affirmation to those who staff largely evening and weekend courses in isolation from their colleagues. At each reception, the college president, in an especially appropriate and visible way, reinforces the importance of the adjunct faculty in achieving the college's overall mission. The reception was provided additional prestige and excitement in 2003, when the first group of Outstanding Adjunct Faculty Members were recognized.

Earlier in the academic year, the Adjunct Faculty Committee had focused its work exclusively on developing the award's objectives, that is, to recognize high performers, provide role models and mentors for future adjunct instructors, and elevate the stature of adjunct instruction, formulating the award's eligibility criteria, and planning its nomination and selection processes. As is often the case, the major challenge of installing the award was ensuring that all stakeholders—

adjunct instructors, department chairs, full-time faculty members, and students—were provided sufficient input into each step and kept appropriately informed of decisions in the design process. As final decisions were made, the committee members concluded that this challenge was successfully managed when the group of award winners selected represented a wide array of discipline areas and all five of the college's campuses. Following their recognition, winners were widely accepted as deserving recipients.

Besides the pride that the winners and their families exuded when their awards were presented, the award's implementation could be seen to foster goodwill among other adjunct instructors in attendance. Additional positive public relations were generated when coverage of the winners appeared in local media outlets and campus publications. While the committee members became aware of modifications they would make in future years, the award was clearly a victory for their work. Attendance at subsequent years' receptions is expected to steadily climb as the Outstanding Faculty Member Award achieves wider exposure.

Information Resources

The final component of the adjunct faculty professional development initiative was the creation of a professional development information resource that could be accessed by individuals as needed. Initially housed in an instructional dean's office, a growing collection of books was centralized several years later in the campus library to provide greater access and convenience. The August 2003 adjunct faculty survey indicated that a better effort needs to be made to promote awareness of this resource, as only 28% of respondents had used it.

As the college web site evolved, a professional development page was added that included links to online resources that would appeal to all instructors—new and veteran, full- and part-time. In addition, frequently asked questions (FAQs), with hyperlinks to key sections of the adjunct faculty handbook and additional resources especially for adjunct instructors, were posted and continue to be added and updated. The survey indicated that just over 60% of respondents had accessed the web page and that 76% of these found it to be useful. Making this resource even more inviting and valuable to adjunct instructors will have the additional benefit of encouraging integration of technology into their own instructional practices.

Summary and Conclusions

Shortly after its inception, this low-cost initiative began to show significant improvements in the teaching and classroom management skills of its participants and began to foster a stronger sense of community among the division's faculty members. Instructional leaders in other divisions began to employ some of its components, especially the Instructor Effectiveness Training course, for both adjunct and new full-time faculty members, and to adapt other components within their instructional units. Increasing opportunities for full- and part-timers to talk on a collegial level mushroomed, and the bifurcation between full- and part-time faculty members that was cited so widely in *The Invisible Faculty* (Gappa & Leslie, 1993) and had previously existed at IRCC, began to erode. Within a year, the disparaging remarks about part-time faculty members that had once been embarrassingly common became increasingly rare. Adjunct instructors became more evident on campus, frequently stopping by their instructional departments to get updated on critical issues and discuss teaching and classroom management strategies with full-timers. The end-of-year reception became an event that full-time faculty members and administrators genuinely looked forward to attending, and one in which they became more openly and genuinely engaged with their part-time colleagues. Increasingly, adjunct instructors were being viewed as a resource that enabled the college to teach effective evening and weekend courses to demanding adult students, extending the reach and influence of the college (Lyons, 1999).

Since their inception a century ago, community colleges have prided themselves as strong teaching institutions for the first-generation students that they largely serve and with whom an impact can be so significant (Rodriguez, 2001). Since their beginnings, community colleges have employed professionals from the communities they serve to provide expertise in critical areas, mitigate fluctuations in enrollment, to staff course sections at difficult times and places, and to control costs (Gappa & Leslie, 1993). While some want to perceive a disparity in teaching quality between full- and part-time faculty members, research continues to find few or no differences (Leslie & Gappa, 2002). During the tight budget times expected to extend well into the future, community colleges will no doubt employ as many or more part-time instructors to staff their courses than before. In an age when legislators, students, their employers and parents, and financial aid providers are expecting increased instructional quality and accountability, community colleges can no longer afford to provide greater support to full-time faculty members without doing the same for its increasingly critical part-timers (Lyons, 2004).

This chapter has sought to provide a valid and objective view of one community college's effort to address these issues proactively. While some elements of the IRCC model may well be a good fit for other institutions, it is important that each college examine closely its unique situation relative to adjunct faculty, ask the difficult questions that run the risk of making many within the institution challenge their existing paradigms, and devise a strategy for more fully integrating better prepared adjunct instructors into the full range of their cultures. It is in the best long-term interest of all stakeholders in each community college to do so.

References

Gappa, J. M., & Leslie, D. W. (1993). *The invisible faculty: Improving the status of part-timers in higher education.* San Francisco, CA: Jossey-Bass.

Leslie, D. W., & Gappa, J. M. (2002). Part-time faculty: Competent and committed. In C. L. Outcalt (Ed.), *New directions for community colleges: No. 118. Community college faculty: Characteristics, practices, and challenges* (pp. 59–67). San Francisco, CA: Jossey-Bass.

Lyons, R. E. (1996). A study of the effects of a mentoring initiative on the performance of new adjunct community college faculty (Doctoral dissertation, University of Central Florida, 1996). *Dissertation Abstracts International, 57,* 4243.

Lyons, R. E. (1999). Adjunct faculty: A priceless resource. *Community College Week, 11*(13), 4, 16.

Lyons, R. E. (2004). *Success strategies for adjunct faculty.* Boston, MA: Allyn & Bacon.

Lyons, R. E., Kysilka, M. L., & Pawlas, G. W. (1999). *The adjunct professor's guide to success: Surviving and thriving in the college classroom.* Boston, MA: Allyn & Bacon.

Rodriguez, S. (2001). *Giants among us: First generation students who lead activist lives.* Nashville, TN: Vanderbilt University Press.

Roueche, J. E., Roueche, S. D., & Milliron, M. D. (1995). *Strangers in their own land: Part-time faculty in American community colleges.* Washington, DC: Community College Press.

Appendix 8A

Instructor Effectiveness Training
MNA 1330

Class: Saturday mornings, 8:30–12 noon
B building, room 111, Fort Pierce Campus
One credit course, satisfies portion of recertification requirement

Textbook: *The Adjunct Professor's Guide to Success* (new adjuncts) or *Success Strategies for Adjunct Faculty* (veterans), or *Teaching College in an Age of Accountability* (full-timers), available at the IRCC Bookstore, or at *Amazon.com* or *BN.com.* A three-ring notebook is recommended for organizing handout materials that will be provided. Additional complimentary resources are available at www.developfaculty.com.

Instructor: Dr. Richard Lyons received his B.S. in business administration and M.A. in marketing education from Western Kentucky University and his Ed.D. in curriculum and instruction from the University of Central Florida. He began teaching college courses as an adjunct instructor at WKU, following work as a supermarket manager and in sales. He has been at IRCC since 1987, as adjunct then full-time instructor, then later as department chair and instructional dean.

Office: Dr. Lyons will be available following the end of each class meeting in B 117. He may be reached at school (462-4715) or from Martin & Indian River counties (1-866-866-4715) or best by email (rlyons@ircc.edu).

Teaching Methods: A wide variety of instructional methods will be used to provide you with meaningful learning experiences, and to provide a model for you to adapt for your classes. These include group problem solving and self-analysis instruments, as well as more traditional methods.

Objectives: Upon completion of this course, each participant will be able to:
1) Explain the function of the department chair
2) Develop an effective course syllabus
3) Describe the factors impacting the success of community college students
4) Conduct an effective first class meeting
5) Explain prudent classroom organizational skills
6) Demonstrate a variety of instructional methodologies
7) Plan, conduct, and follow-up field trips and guest presentations
8) Identify the factors impacting professionalism in the classroom
9) Demonstrate transactional analysis techniques
10) Compare and contrast test formats
11) Analyze test results, take corrective actions
12) Conduct formal and informal student evaluations
13) Explain frequently misunderstood college policies and procedures

Attendance Policy: Although the instructor is providing opportunities for each participant's achievement of course objectives, please recognize the value that your experiences and insights offer others as well. Therefore, it is critical that you attend and participate actively in each session. An "S" will not be awarded to any student missing more than one class.

Grading   Attendance, participation
Criteria: Journal (standard provided), minimum of six entries

Schedule

Session 1   **Planning the Course**   *APG 4 & 5, SSAF 3 & 4*
The 7 Habits of Highly Effective Instructors
Utilizing your most critical resource: the department chair
Resources for planning: textbook, ancillaries, media, course
    outlines
Today's community college student
Developing an effective syllabus—your contract with students
Preparing for the first class meeting

Session 2   **Managing Your Course Effectively**   *APG 6 & 7, SSAF 5 & 6*
Introducing yourself effectively to the class
Using icebreakers and student profiles effectively
Establishing an appropriate atmosphere, professionalism
Effective communications techniques, transactional analysis
Managing class time effectively
Dealing with common teaching challenges

Session 3   **Maximizing Teaching Effectiveness**   *APG 8 & 9, SSAF 7 & 8*
Dovetailing instruction and evaluation
Asking questions, lecturing effectively
Using field trips, guest speakers, and other activities effectively
Cooperative and experiential learning
Using audiovisual materials and equipment effectively
Infusing technology into your instruction

Session 4   **Evaluating Success**   *APG, SSAF 10, 11 & 13*
*Journals due
Comparing and contrasting test formats
Exam construction, de-bugging
Scoring exams, using Scantron system, analyzing test results
Students' and peers' assessments of teaching: informal and formal
Closing questions, discussion

PART THREE

Supporting Part-Time Faculty Through Technology

9 | SUPPORTING AND SUSTAINING ADJUNCT FACULTY WITH 4FACULTY.ORG

Kristina Kauffman

Supporting and sustaining adjunct faculty is not an easy task, but it is vital to the success of community colleges and the students they serve. Adjuncts need professional development experiences that provide the tools for success in the community college teaching environment. They also need a sense of community—a view that they are a vital and integral part of the community that makes up the college. Outside these two common needs, as Gappa and Leslie (1993) remind us, adjuncts differ dramatically in preparation and in their personal sense of mission.

In California, where the 4faculty.org project was launched, over 30,000 adjuncts serve in 108 colleges, making attention to their needs a logistical nightmare, but extremely necessary. Seeing this need, 4faculty.org began as a way to orient adjunct faculty and proposed the Internet as the delivery method.

Birth of an Idea

Like many projects, the idea germinated from an experience common in community colleges—last-minute hiring. It is common in California for adjunct faculty to be hired days or even hours before a class begins. With a shiny new M.A. in hand (or the appropriate occupational credentials), and absolutely no idea how to manage a college class, most faculty teach the way their favorite professors taught. Those who experienced great teaching and learning opportunities come to community colleges with some good practices, but they rarely have a rationale for their success. Others come with teaching perspectives inappropriate for the complex needs of adult learners in community colleges.

Additionally, adjuncts are rarely given office spaces and opportunities to build strong relationships with their full-time peers. Most are "freeway flyers," using the library or hallways to meet with their students. Often their schedules make interaction with peers nearly impossible, or they are faced with cynical full-time colleagues who refuse to make time to support faculty who may only stay with the college for a year.

The Big Picture

Across the nation there is an unprecedented need to hire more community college faculty to fulfill the demand placed on the college by a new generation of college students with a far greater desire, and financial and geographic ability, to attend college than their parents. In 2003, 75.4% of high-school graduates went to college; in 1979, only 50% enrolled in higher education (Boggs, 2003). In California, a rapid student population growth coupled with faculty retirements has created a huge demand for new faculty (as many as 18,700 in the first decade of the 21st century) to educate the students of the largest system of higher education in the world (Piland & Phillips, 2000). Nationwide adjunct faculty carry more than half of the teaching assignments in most community colleges, yet they receive far less than half of the institutional support. Approximately 80% of community college budgets are spent on personnel wages and benefits. Since adjunct faculty provide half the teaching nationally, they represent a multi-billion dollar investment in people, an investment that must be protected. Highly skilled adjunct faculty members can enrich the curriculum and strengthen the tie between the college and its community. The pool of available adjuncts is decreasing; thus, more and more adjuncts will be relatively new to teaching, making recruitment, professional development, and orientation efforts even more essential.

Most observers agree that the most serious institutional problem community colleges face is the underpreparedness of students who often have significant deficiencies in basic skills. Many of these students are dependent upon effective teaching and learning techniques for their success—techniques many new faculty do not have. Traditional lecture formats that are teacher centered, rather than learner centered, are often disengaging and uninspiring for these students. Faced with frustration and failure, they leave the college before they make any progress. This reality suggests an overwhelming need for high-quality, comprehensive faculty development aimed at the creation of experiences that support underprepared students and optimize student learning. As *The California Master Plan for Education* states,

> Essential to meet this responsibility is faculty knowledge and understanding of instructional and learning processes, the design and development of curriculum, assessment of learning, and identification of student needs. Further, faculty knowledge of and comfort with teaching and learning in diverse classrooms and appropriate integration of technology into teaching and curriculum . . . are critically important to the achievement of all students. Unfortunately, few doctoral programs . . . incorporate preparation in these areas into their core curriculum. (Joint Committee to Develop a Master Plan for Education, 2002, p. 31)

While excellent professional development programs existed in California in the 1990s, most of these programs focused on face-to-face workshops. The schedules maintained by most adjuncts simply do not allow them to attend face-to-face workshops. As a result, most California community colleges had no comprehensive program for adjunct faculty development.

A review of the literature on professional development prior to the creation of 4faculty.org revealed that nationally colleges have a scattered pattern of response to the needs of adjunct faculty. The literature revealed that adjunct faculty development programs were nonexistent or limited to the creation of an adjunct faculty handbook, a variety of face-to-face short-term adjunct faculty events, veteran/adjunct faculty mentoring situations, and/or technology-related orientation programs and mini-training videos. It is not surprising then that adjunct faculty have been described by Roueche, Roueche, and Milliron (1995) as strangers in their own land.

Practical Application

Faculty need to learn the art and science of teaching. High-quality teaching is an intentional art, informed by subject-matter expertise and by scientific research on facilitating learning. Teaching is an art form in that it reflects the personal characteristics, talents, and world-view of the teacher. Outstanding teaching in the 21st century also reflects the science of teaching as it utilizes research-based, scientifically validated methodologies to:

- Engage and support learning for all students
- Create and maintain effective environments for learning
- Organize subject matter; plan instruction and design learning experiences for all learners
- Assess achievement of intended learning outcomes

Learning can take place with or without a teacher. Motivated, intelligent, and skilled students can learn in spite of very bad teaching. However, quality teaching can:

- Enhance the learning experience
- Inspire learners to pursue a subject in greater depth and with greater enthusiasm
- Facilitate the discovery of linkages between the known and the unknown and between the immediate topic and the broader world of knowledge
- Ease the achievement of intended learning outcomes
- Make success possible for underprepared students

4faculty.org began with these goals in mind. They were not fully articulated at the time, but they were a prime motivator. Within a few days of being struck by an inspiring solution to the needs of adjunct faculty at Riverside Community College, a five-page submission to the Fund for the Improvement of Postsecondary Education (FIPSE) was drafted. FIPSE liked the idea and asked that a coalition of colleges be built. Colleagues known to be knowledgeable about professional development were contacted, and a California Community College Chancellor's Office Fund for Student Success grant was written to build a bigger financial base. A "crazy little idea" to help the adjuncts on one campus became a collaboration of hard working, positive people who refined the idea and built 4faculty.org.

4faculty.org

4faculty.org appeared online in the fall of 2001. It was billed as a response to the dramatically increased demand for new adjunct faculty in the community college system and as a cost-effective and convenient approach to orientation and professional development of adjunct faculty. Equally important to the creation of 4faculty.org were the burgeoning developments in online education.

A cohort of 11 colleges in California led by Riverside Community College District's Office of Faculty Affairs—including College of the Desert, Diablo Valley College, Mt. San Antonio College, Pasadena City College, Rio Hondo College, San Diego City College, San Diego Mesa College, San Diego Miramar College, Santa Barbara City College, and Santa Monica College—and more than 200 outstanding faculty, administrators, and technical staff members ultimately produced 4faculty.org.

A substantially revised version of 4faculty.org was launched in September 2002, containing more diverse content, expanded technology modules, more practical tips, and dynamically driven pages allowing for greater customization.

Inside 4faculty.org

Developed by topic area experts, 4faculty.org provides comprehensive professional development modules and tools to help faculty reach students more effectively and enhance their learning experience. Faculty of member institutions may set up a personalized account and select from 26 content modules, or they may opt for one of two set tracks: a full new-faculty orientation or a series of modules for veteran faculty. They may also choose a three-hour quick introduction to their college and community college teaching. Additionally, six modules are specifically designed for new clinical nursing faculty. Future plans include content related to accreditation, leadership and occupational education issues, in addition to many more templates and tips.

The course allows faculty members to gain the knowledge necessary to succeed from their first day in class. It provides tools and techniques as faculty plan their first lessons, and leads new faculty through the maze of issues they will address, such as how to establish learning objectives, create informative syllabi, make a positive first impression, address various learning styles, and use technology effectively. In addition, it provides advice for dealing with the heterogeneous student bodies of the community college system, various state legal requirements, and unique college policies. 4faculty.org also includes technical and pedagogical advice, information about how people learn, and how to communicate effectively with large groups and individual students.

Each module includes a pathway for learning titled the DREAM system. "D" stands for Discover, where readers find a brief introduction to the topic and its relevance, as well as learning objectives. "R" indicates the Read section, where users may find reading materials, interactive items, or video presentations designed by the authors of this course. An expert or team of experts in the topic area wrote each "reading." These materials are presented using the best practices in online course design:

- Introducing information in a user-friendly format employing numerous headings, lists where applicable, boxes with definitions, and graphics to make it easier to remember the information

- Providing context by illustrating how knowledge of the subject may be useful to your life outside the class today or in the future
- Accommodating various types of learners by using visually stimulating materials and audio readings for each lesson

Due to the amount of information contained in modules, there are often multiple sub-pages within the "Read" section. Many read sections also contain "Dig Deeper" links to more in-depth information written by the course authors. The third section, "Explore," includes recommended books, journal articles, and web sites. The authors have carefully selected these references and they represent only works for which they offer a strong recommendation. The "Apply" section offers tips on how to apply what was learned in each module into the classroom, lab, or on the campus. Users are encouraged to make contributions to this section. Finally, in the "Measure" section, users are asked to pause and reflect upon what they have learned in the module, and to respond to a set of multiple-choice questions that assess knowledge acquisition based upon specific references in the read sections, as well as broadly assess general understanding of the module's content. Many member colleges offer professional development credit based upon successful passage of this quiz. The modules offered are:

- 100–Quick Start Guide for Community College Faculty
- 101–History and Mission of Community Colleges
- 102–Introduction to Your College
- 103–Characteristics of Community Colleges and Their Students
- 104–Preparing for the 1st Day of Class
- 105–Building Your Syllabus
- 106–Assessment
- 107–Grades and Testing
- 108–Effective Class Management
- 109–How People Learn
- 110–Learning Theories
- 111–Approaches to Teaching
- 112–Technology in the Classroom
- 113–Technology and Distance Education
- 114–Legal & Ethical Issues in the Digital Information Age

- 115–Increasing Effective Communication and Student Resiliency
- 116 - Helping Your Students
- 117–Student Support Services
- 118–Focusing on Diverse Needs
- 119–How College Governance Affects You
- 120–Surviving the Journey
- 201–NURSING–Role Transition
- 202–NURSING–Getting Started
- 203–NURSING–Teaching Clinical: The Process
- 204–NURSING–Evaluation
- 205–NURSING–Legal/Ethical Issues
- 206–NURSING–Promoting Critical Thinking in Clinical Settings

The team that created 4faculty.org operated with the belief that improving faculty understanding of teaching and learning will improve the quality of instruction. Or as Boggs (2003) suggested, "Improved instruction, and particularly increased student involvement through the use of learner-focused techniques, would result in decreased dropout rates, increased learning, and higher completion of student educational goals."

Research Results

4faculty.org is independently evaluated by Shel Bockman and Barbara Sirotnik of the Institute of Applied Research at California State University–San Bernardino. Their research findings give insight into what adjunct faculty experience and what type of support they need. All faculty in the study were new to their college or campus. In the research, faculty were asked some general information related to prior teaching experiences and whether they received any assistance *other* than the 4faculty.org online course.

The majority of adjunct faculty (80.7%) who were new to their college/campus indicated prior teaching experience, and two-thirds (67.2%) had taught for more than one year. Of those, three out of four had some prior teaching experience in higher education, and 12% had industry or military/government trainer experience. Despite their experience only 49.2% reported that they were very confident as an instructor.

A questionnaire was designed to assess the specific areas where faculty feel they need more preparation for teaching (see Table 9.1). Interestingly faculty seem to be suggesting that they are prepared for the mechanics of teaching: syllabi construction and communication with their students. Yet their post 4faculty.org feedback would suggest otherwise. After completing 4faculty.org, 80% said that they would modify the way they teach (or planned to teach) based on the information received from this online course. More specifically, they will clarify learning objectives, improve syllabi design, expand communication skills, and enhance assessment tools as a result of their experience with 4faculty.org. Early results from 4faculty.org's beta test found that 96% of faculty reported the course to be "very helpful" or "somewhat helpful."

TABLE 9.1
AREAS WHERE FACULTY REPORT THEY NEED MORE PREPARATION FOR TEACHING

	Percent
In knowledge of support services available to you	81.6%
In techniques for motivating students	76.8%
In knowledge of support services available to students	75.6%
In the use of technology as a teaching tool	74.3%
In dealing with various student learning styles	72.7%
In college policies and procedures	72.1%
To use a variety of teaching methods	69.5%
In methods to evaluate student learning	69.2%
In dealing with students who are underrepresented	63.2%
To organize delivery of the curriculum	57.1%
To deal with various student classroom disruptions and emergencies	56.2%
In techniques for structuring class time	54.3%
To construct a syllabus	37.5%
In communication skills	33.0%

4faculty.org's research project revealed some other interesting results related to adjunct faculty's level of connectedness to the college. More than 60% of adjunct faculty expressed an interest in faculty social activities and other campus activities such as sports, musicals, and plays. Even more (87.3%) expressed interest in curriculum development and committee and department activities (78.5%). This finding disputes the notion that adjunct faculty are not deeply interested in the academic programs at their colleges. Adjuncts may be thought of as "freeway flyers" (at least in California), but clearly they have an interest in the academic health of their college and departments and are interesting in participating. Yet, barely a majority suggest that they are familiar with their college and its services (see Table 9.2).

Outside of their interest in their college, faculty reported that they wanted to learn more about teaching in the community college environment, including how they might increase their productivity and serve adult learners. Most noted their interest in enhancing or improving teaching skills, particularly relating to updated methods, teaching strategies, learning styles, classroom dynamics, and themselves as a faculty member.

- "I really wanted to know more about teaching. Anything that can help me. It's pretty scary teaching part-time, you get thrown into it."
- "I have never had an education course and I was teaching. I thought, there's got to be a lot of things I could learn."

4faculty.org's authors and editors were pleased with initial faculty feedback. Included in the research findings were comments such as:

TABLE 9.2
FACULTY FAMILIARITY WITH THE COLLEGE

	Familiar	Not Familiar
The history of the college	51.7%	48.3%
The mission of the college	69.3%	30.7%
Faculty support services	49.4%	50.6%
Student support services	57.4%	42.6%

- "It was/is practical advice that relates specifically to the quality of my teaching."
- " . . . I was also impressed with the amount of information and resources provided concerning student success and feel that I will refer to that information often."

Faculty reported that they will be altering their teaching. While responses varied they included:

- "I will be paying attention to my natural learning/teaching style, and adapt my teaching style such that students of all learning styles can learn effectively from me."
- "What I learned about learning patterns helped me immensely in planning my classroom time more effectively. . . . I am still working on changes at every class based on what I have learned in this program."

Faculty mentioned changes they would make, including use of "some of the lecture techniques, icebreakers, and observation questions," and multi-sensory methods of teaching. Importantly they also recognized the need to be more structured and organized.

Perhaps the most rewarding comment for 4faculty.org authors came from a Ph.D. in English, Lisa Rodriguez from Mt. San Antonio College:

- "It's the best thing that ever happened to me. I spent $50,000 on graduate school and learned nothing about how to teach college students. This course just saved me."

In fact, Lisa was so inspired by the project she ultimately joined the team of authors from Mt. San Antonio and contributed to the web site.

The majority of faculty mentioned specific lessons or sections that they felt were the most useful part of the course. Faculty ranked "Planning your First Class" highest among available lessons:

- " . . . [it] dealt with the actual process of putting together class materials and presentations."

Faculty mentioned the section on syllabus construction as a very useful tool and that "Helping Students Succeed in Your Course" also proved valuable. As one faculty member stated:

- "Some students may need a little help to get through a course; others may need to build more skills. Being able to recognize students with more needs early in the semester may help them to complete the course."

Not surprisingly "Approaches to Teaching" also gained favorable reviews.

"Surviving the Journey," which was almost an afterthought by the editors, surprised its authors by gaining many positive comments including:

- " . . . reminded me that I need to work on keeping things in balance."

Another faculty member pointed out the importance of dealing with potential crisis issues, such as students with possible emotional problems or violent tendencies:

- "No one addressed this area in any of the teaching courses I have taken."

Faculty also expressed appreciation for the links to various resources.

The majority of faculty rated 4faculty.org as either "very helpful" (55.1%) or "somewhat helpful" (37.7%). Only 7.2% said the course was "not very helpful," and no one rated it as "not at all helpful," suggesting that the vast majority of adjuncts appreciated having 4faculty.org and felt they and their students benefited from professional development efforts. Faculty were asked if they intend to modify the way they teach (or plan to teach) as a result of taking the online course. Most of the responses focused on two main issues: the various learning styles and needs of students and the faculty member's own teaching style. The following comments more clearly illustrate these two approaches:

- "I am much more aware of the student and that I need to evaluate where they are at and ensure that I focus on them much more and how I can deliver the lesson to their understanding."
- "I think it has helped me realize how to communicate better and listen to the students. Try to involve them and realize that they learn by participating more rather than I'm just talking at them."

In addition, some of the faculty indicated that they will incorporate more technology into their courses, specifically in terms of more use of the Internet and email to communicate with students. Finally, faculty said they will modify the way they evaluate and assess their students.

Even for faculty who indicated that they have no plans to modify their teaching based on the material learned in 4faculty.org, their follow-up responses seem to suggest otherwise. Simply put, the online course has reinforced their pedagogical approach. In these cases subcontextual analysis suggests that the course had more of an impact on faculty than they might have explicitly acknowledged. Consider the anecdotal evidence in the following quotes:

- "The course actually gave me positive reinforcement about what I am currently doing. So in this way it was helpful in letting me know I am going in the right direction. I can thus concentrate on doing better what I am already doing."
- "It was incredibly and surprisingly helpful. For a first year faculty person, it should be required for them. It should be in the contract. There's an assumption that you have the credentials . . . it's ripping off our students to assume that people with credentials and a personality can teach. 4faculty covers what you need to do to help your students succeed and to help you succeed. There's no question that my students will benefit from my taking this course."

Summary and Conclusions

The lessons learned through 4faculty.org have been many and varied. They include the following:

- Community colleges need professional development at every level.
- Professional development must be timely, accessible, and relevant.
- Professional development can lead to improved teaching and learning.
- Professional development can be cost effective.

Community colleges reflect the communities they serve. Like all governmental agencies they face a series of challenges including the ongoing need for leadership and succession planning, strategic human capital planning, organizational alignment to recruit and develop staff whose size, skills, and deployment meet agency needs, and creating a results-oriented organizational climate (U.S. Department of Labor, 2003). Going beyond these broader challenges, community colleges must develop current and future leaders and staff committed to change, organizational development, and learning. To accomplish this, community colleges need to identify, find support for, and measure work that facilitates learning; acquire and develop staff and faculty who facilitate learning; and create a results-oriented climate focused on learning.

4faculty.org's original purpose was to promote excellent instruction for increasing diverse and underprepared students, bring adjunct faculty into the campus community more quickly and effectively, and increase student success and retention. In addition, 4faculty.org now provides faculty with tools to facilitate learning, helps faculty understand how to measure learning, and serves as a useful tool for recruiting and intern programs. 4faculty.org reaches faculty with various schedules in locations of convenience to them. It provides resources that are timely and that do not get lost in piles of paper, ensuring that vital reference documents are available 24/7 wherever faculty and administration may need them.

4faculty.org's experience has shown that professional development can have a positive impact on faculty behavior. The majority of new adjunct faculty rewrote syllabi, were more creative in their approach to teaching, enhanced their communication skills, shared their newfound knowledge of student services, and better understood their own career planning options. The experience showed that faculty really do want to know more about their own college, that faculty want professional development resources to be tightly designed and efficiently delivered, and that faculty appreciate tangible tools for their classes. In short, when colleges provide opportunities for easily accessible information about excellent instruction and promoting student success, adjunct faculty will benefit.

While targeted professional development is critical if faculty are to serve today's students, funding for professional development is often the first thing cut in difficult financial times—a decision that may be more expensive over time. Dropouts and failure rates are costly. If faculty are able to help just one more student succeed each year than they had in the past due to professional development efforts, then the small cost of professional development would more than pay for itself in student success—a significant savings to a system. Of course, it is too soon to know for certain if these results are achievable or sustainable over time, but the experience with 4faculty.org suggests these questions should be asked.

Adjunct faculty regularly report that belonging to a college community is important to their success. Offering 4faculty.org, integrated with college-specific information, gives adjunct faculty an opportunity to understand the college community and policies. It is a first step in suggesting that what adjuncts do is valuable and that they too need support and development services. In addition, they want administrative support and recognition, work space to meet with students, access to computers, campus networks, email, listservs, and directory listings. In short, they want the very same services that full-time faculty demand, and often take for granted. They may also be interested in playing a role in decision-making and planning for quality instruction. Many departments have sequential programs requiring coherence between all faculty, yet part- timers are not paid to attend meetings. Budgetary and legal constraints, not to mention the huge demands placed on the system as student needs increase, make it very difficult, if not impossible, to provide the individualized services and rewards adjunct faculty crave. Yet merely acknowledging the issues and sincerely desiring to support part-time faculty to the highest level possible can go a long way to build trust and community.

As the pool of well-qualified adjunct faculty continues to decline, community colleges will find themselves in competition for highly skilled part-time faculty. Colleges attentive to the intangibles in tough times are likely to reap the benefits of better faculty down the road. It is a wise investment in our colleges and in the future quality of education for our students.

References

Boggs, G. R. (2003, November 21). *Keynote.* Paper presented at the annual conference of the Community College League of California.

Gappa, J. M., & Leslie, D. W. (1993). *The invisible faculty: Improving the status of part-timers in higher education.* San Francisco, CA: Jossey-Bass.

Joint Committee to Develop a Master Plan for Education. (2002). *The California master plan for education.* Retrieved June 25, 2004, from http://www.sen.ca.gov/ftp/SEN/COMMITTEE/JOINT/ MASTER_PLAN/_home/020909_FINAL_MASTER_PLAN_ DOCUMENTS/2002_FINAL_COMPLETEMASTER PLAN_2.PDF

Piland, W., & Phillips, B. (2000, August). *Long-range administrator needs projections: Preparing the next generation of community college leaders—facilitating institutional development.* Paper prepared for the California Community College Chancellor's Office, Sacramento, CA.

Roueche, J. E., Roueche, S. D., & Milliron, M. D. (1995). *Strangers in their own land: Part-time faculty in American community colleges.* Washington, DC: Community College Press.

U.S. Department of Labor. (2003). *Building a model workplace for the 21st century: Human capital strategic plan, 2003–2008.* Washington, DC: Author. Retrieved June 25, 2004, from http://www.dol.gov/_ sec/stratplan/2003/humancapital/hcstrategic_plan.pdf

10 | SUPPORTING ADJUNCT FACULTY AS IF THE COLLEGE'S LIFE DEPENDED ON IT

Deborah Stewart and Rebecca Werner

In community colleges today, adjunct instructors often teach a majority of classes. At the Community College of Vermont (CCV), part-time instructors teach 100% of the courses. As a result, CCV has developed innovative methods to support its more than 700 instructors. In particular, CCV focuses much of its energy on new instructors—instructors who are new to CCV and who may or may not be new to teaching altogether—since this provides the college with the opportunity to reach them at a critical point in their development. For example, although CCV instructors are often specialists in a particular field of study, they may not be familiar with classroom teaching for adult students. Additionally, the mental models that many veteran instructors bring to the classroom may consist of highly traditional teaching methods—often the same methods they themselves experienced as students. To support and encourage the development of these instructors, CCV begins by frontloading its training with a required three-hour orientation called Great Beginnings, in which instructors are introduced—through classroom activities and a handbook—to the practical and philosophical aspects of teaching at the community college.

An Overview of CCV

CCV was founded in 1970 to bring higher education to the people of Vermont in their local communities. Today the college serves more than 5,500 students each semester (more than 8500 annually), making its enrollment the second largest of any college in Vermont. CCV is an open-admissions, two-year institution serving the educational needs of students through daytime, evening, weekend, and online offerings in 12 communities throughout the state. It provides credit courses, certificate programs, degree programs, and continuing educational opportunities. In addition, CCV is one of five institutions in the Vermont State Colleges system working together toward a common mission: "For the benefit of Vermont, the Vermont State Colleges provide affordable, high quality, student-centered and accessible education, fully integrating professional, liberal and career study" (Vermont State Colleges, 2004).

Students

Ninety-six percent of CCV students are Vermonters, and most are among the first in their families to attend college. While nearly three-quarters of students are seeking a degree, most attend college part-time (only 13% are enrolled full-time). One-third of the students are new to college each semester, and slightly less than one-half arrive at CCV academically under-prepared.

CCV believes it's important to help students become self-reliant people who know how to learn individually and through cooperation with others. When students leave the college, they need to be effective learners and citizens who have built a strong foundation of academic, critical thinking, and collaborative skills, which they can then use to learn a new subject, adapt to changing circumstances, and fulfill their career and personal aspirations. Because education at CCV is integrally connected to the transformation of students as learners, the college encourages instructors to plan and teach their subjects in ways that provide these opportunities for students.

Instructors

More than 700 part-time instructors teach every semester. Some have never taught a college class before coming to CCV. Others are seasoned veterans with years of experience at CCV or other institutions. Many are working professionals who generously share their passion for a subject or vocation with students who are equally passionate about learning. Also, a number of instructors are staff members who teach in addition to their full-time responsibilities with the college.

Knowing who instructors are and what they want from teaching is akin to knowing who students are and what they want from learning. Both are critically important to making a college work as a teaching and learning institution. CCV recognized early on that providing instructors with support, encouragement, and opportunities for professional growth best serve the work of a learning college (O'Banion, 1997).

Academic Coordinators

CCV instructors and students are supported by about 130 full-time staff. Each of the 12 site offices has a core academic and office staff. The key academic staff members in each location are the coordinators of academic services, a role that is virtually unique in higher education. Coordinators plan course offerings for each semester, recruit and select part-time faculty to teach those courses, and advise students on all matters related to their program and course selection.

The title "coordinator" conveys the essential task of this role. Coordinators bring students and instructors together in classrooms where genuine learning occurs; in effect, coordinators are the glue that holds CCV together as a networked system of learning communities. The coordinator holds both the students' and instructors' views and interests in mind and thus can be an effective mediator should a difficulty or challenge arise in the classroom. Furthermore, while coordinators mentor students in the educational process, they also mentor instructors. Many coordinators arrive at the role through their expertise as instructors, and nearly 80% of coordinators continue to teach in addition to their full-time commitment to the college. One of the reasons CCV can continue to operate with a 100% part-time faculty is because it has nearly 50 full-time coordinators who directly support the teaching and learning process around the state.

Great Beginnings: An Orientation to Teaching at CCV

While nearly two-thirds of instructors have taught at least two years at CCV, a significant number (generally 10%–15%) are new each semester. Early on, CCV saw the new instructor experience—with all its capacity for development—as an opportunity to connect with instructors on the practical and philosophical aspects of being in a classroom. This led to modeling the Great Beginnings workshop after a typical CCV class. The workshop runs for a three-hour session, so facilitators can model the behaviors of an effective college teacher and illustrate firsthand how a session of that length can be active and engaging. Likewise, CCV has designed a three-week online session to model active learning in the online environment.

Initially, training for new instructors was integrated into statewide semiannual instructor conferences. However, the demand was just too great. Besides moving the orientation to all 12 of its sites and online, the college decided it would be most effective if the workshop were scheduled for three to six weeks before the semester began, since this is when instructors are doing their most intensive preparations. Once delivery was set, facilitators began teaching and assessing the orientation. Since 90% of all new instructors were participating in the orientation on a voluntary basis, CCV made the orientation a contractual obligation for teaching. Thus, the college is able to ensure that all instructors enter the classroom with some knowledge about CCV, its students, and good practices for teaching.

From the start, the responsibility for designing and teaching the orientation lay with the academic dean's office and instructor development committee. Even today, when more than 30 of these workshops are held each year, statewide and online, they are so important to the college's overall work of supporting instructors that they continue to be facilitated by the academic dean, two associate deans, and several academic coordinators.

Goals of Great Beginnings

The goals of Great Beginnings include exploring the college's educational philosophy, examining the diversity of its student population, demonstrating a variety of teaching methods and classroom management strategies, discussing assessment procedures, preparing instructors to deliver an effective first-class session, responding to instructors' own questions and concerns, and generating enthusiasm for the coming term. In addition, facilitators work to meet these goals without relying on a didactic model of delivery.

Exploring the College's Educational Philosophy

CCV developed a set of principles that describes how instructors can best serve the learning needs of students (see Figure 10.1). Not only do the Principles of Good Teaching and Learning provide a set of values for teaching at CCV, but they shape the way students will evaluate the instruction in their courses. At the end of every semester, students complete a feedback form that addresses these values. Facilitators introduce the principles in much the same way an instructor might introduce course expectations or an assignment rubric in his or her class. In addition, instructors are first asked to reflect on their own educational experiences and values. The principles are then linked to that discussion. CCV wants instructors to develop a framework for thinking about their work in the classroom *before* they enter it.

Examining the Diversity of Its Student Population

Access lies at the heart of the mission, and CCV strives to remove as many barriers as possible. Many special populations that might be underserved at campus-based colleges dealing primarily with young students are the "traditional" students here. As a result, like other community colleges, CCV attracts both adult students and a growing number of younger students, some of whom are still enrolled in high school. The college has also seen an influx of refugee and immigrant students in many of its sites. While 70% of students are female, males are increasingly interested in pursuing their degrees at CCV. The

FIGURE 10.1
THE PRINCIPLES OF GOOD TEACHING AND LEARNING

The best teaching and learning occurs when:

- **The classroom climate is one of mutual respect among all participants.** It is a primary responsibility of CCV instructors to foster and exhibit respect for all students in the classroom, to hear every student's voice, especially those who have been silenced in previous educational settings. Respect involves a recognition of different points of view, different values, different styles of learning, different talents, and different kinds of intelligence.

- **Students are motivated.** The stronger the desire to learn something, the more learning will occur. Instructors who display genuine passion for their subject matter and communicate high standards can generate a similar enthusiasm among students. Love of learning is the strongest motivation we can provide to our students.

- **The learning environment in the classroom is treated as a holistic, dynamic system designed to accommodate different ways of learning and knowing.** Instructional methods should promote a cycle of learning that includes opportunities for direct hands-on experience; for reflection through reading, writing, and discussion; for students to derive personal meaning or make connections to their daily lives; and for discovering direct applications for the learning. The deepest learning states often occur when the whole brain is engaged, when analytical left-brain processes are accompanied by a range of right-brain understandings.

- **Content is presented with the big picture first as a context for the specific, differentiated information of the subject.** The most meaningful learning generally occurs when students have a context for specific content they are trying to learn. One of the most important aspects of the learning process is that information, material, and activities have to be grounded and connected either to the abstract conceptions that make sense of them or to the students' personal lives. Otherwise any learning that occurs tends to be superficial and/or of short duration.

- **The class encourages dialogue and collaboration among students as well as between students and the instructor.** Dialogue among classroom participants allows for the integration of new knowledge with what students already know, which in turn generates further understandings and fresh insights. Interactions among students and teachers can be the most effective triggers of meaningful learning.

- **The class provides opportunities for direct experience and active application of course content.** Students generally learn things best if they experience them firsthand or apply them directly to solve a problem. Providing students with opportunities to teach others what they are learning is one of the most effective ways to accomplish this kind of applied learning in the classroom.

- **Student development and transformation is an intentional goal of the teaching and learning process.** Student development involves positive changes in the students' frames of reference and their ability to think critically and abstractly. This transformation is most likely to occur in an environment that includes safety and trust and provides occasional experiences of cognitive dissonance or disequilibrium (i.e., experiences that lead students to question their own taken-for-granted beliefs and frames of reference).

- **Assessment is an ongoing process that provides prompt feedback to students about their learning.** Assessment is most effective when there is the least anxiety and the maximum potential to learn from the assessment procedure. Hence, assessment should be perceived by students as a natural and ongoing part of the cycle of learning.

population of students with disabilities has increased five-fold since 1988. Currently, 6% of all students have a documented disability, including, but not limited to, visual and hearing impairments, mobility, psychological and learning disabilities.

The fact is that most classes contain a kaleidoscopic mix of student age levels, backgrounds, learning styles, educational experiences, and motivations. In order to get instructors thinking about the ways that diversity can affect their teaching, facilitators in Great Beginnings ask them to brainstorm on the types of diversity they might encounter in a classroom. This exercise encourages instructors to challenge their assumptions about students. As the brainstorming goes on, the individualism of all students emerges.

This exercise also provides instructors with the opportunity to discuss strategies for addressing some of the challenges in working with a diverse group of students. How might they assess students' knowledge or relevant experience in the first few classes? How might peer teaching or small-group activities engender a successful learning experience for all? And what about presenting students with a choice of assignments, all equally valid but different?

While students differ in many ways, it is important for instructors to emphasize that there is no single model for success in any academic or career field. Excellent students, like excellent teachers, come in all varieties. Since no one speaks more eloquently on the issues of students than students themselves, facilitators present a 10- minute video in the workshop that showcases six students' stories. By embracing the diversity in the classroom, instructors can resist making assumptions that cost time and energy; instead, they can build on the wisdom and strength of the class as a whole and work toward developing a true learning community.

Demonstrating a Variety of Teaching Methods and Classroom Management Strategies

While lecture may be the primary mode of teaching in some institutions, it is not so at CCV. Here, instructors are strongly encouraged to consider student engagement in thinking about their methodology. Learning at CCV is seen as a way of building knowledge and skills, making essential connections, and, therefore, facilitators spend a great deal of time in the orientation illustrating and practicing the strategies that support this. Since students prefer, on the whole, to interact with other students, the instructor, and the course material, it makes sense for instructors to use strategies that promote learning and make it enjoyable.

Active learning strategies engage students in the learning process, especially around the skills of analysis and synthesis. CCV's instructor handbook provides additional ways to energize the classroom, including designing in-class writing prompts, posing problems or application questions, allowing for peer teaching opportunities, and using games. The handbook also provides tips for making the online classroom an active and engaged one, starting with the formation of questions and including the use of ancillary web resources. Most importantly, perhaps, facilitators work diligently in both the on-ground and online orientation to model active learning strategies, illustrating how the classroom can come alive for learners.

Discussing Assessment and Feedback Procedures

Effective instructors use a variety of both assessment and evaluation techniques in their classes. Feedback is essential to helping everyone grow in a teaching and learning institution. For new instructors, in particular, it is important to discuss the merits of and methods for assessment in the classroom. In Great Beginnings, facilitators emphasize the role assessment plays in developing communication between students and instructors. Because assessment in the classroom is often informal and/or anonymous, it's a valuable way for instructors to gauge the effectiveness of certain teaching methods or the absorption of specific content. Using formative classroom assessments on a regular basis is critical to both fostering learning and guiding students toward meeting the objectives of a course (Angelo & Cross, 1994).

Instructors can also simultaneously assess and provide feedback on their students' performance in a class. For instance, an instructor may point out insightful comments made by a particular student or may observe students at work during small-group exercises and offer immediate feedback on their performance. This kind of feedback is especially effective because it is direct, timely, and positively focused.

Preparing Instructors to Deliver an Effective First-Class Session

The first weeks of class are an important time for instructors and students. It is vital to set norms, articulate expectations, develop rapport, assess students' knowledge about a subject, and introduce new information or skills. For students, beginning a class can be a risky and intimidating process. They may feel isolated and ill at ease. They may imagine everyone knows more than they do about a subject. Even the most excited and confident student may entertain thoughts of dropping a course at the slightest hint of "failure" or difficulty. There are, however, ways of building students' interest and commitment at the beginning of a semester. At the same time, these methods can help instructors to gain confidence and fluency in their own teaching.

Since the Great Beginnings orientation acts as a first class of sorts for the instructors who attend, facilitators use the workshop to model some methods for promoting engagement and commitment. To begin, instructors are asked to introduce themselves and to reflect on their experiences as learners. This exercise is then used to connect instructors to the "subject"—effective teaching—which they work on in small groups. Facilitators also articulate expectations by going over the goals or objectives for the workshop. Finally, facilitators end the session by asking instructors to anonymously write questions and comments about the orientation. As facilitators go along, they ask instructors to analyze why they might have presented or framed an exercise in the way they did. For example, they might ask: What are the benefits of working in a small group at this stage in the "class"? What are the challenges for a teacher in doing this? This allows instructors to consider how they might adapt a facilitator's methods for use in their own classrooms.

Responding to Questions and Concerns of Instructors

Part of modeling effective behaviors in the classroom is allowing instructors themselves to shape the direction of certain discussions. Just as it is important to give students in a classroom the opportunity to own their learning, facilitators work hard in the Great Beginnings orientation to engage instructors and encourage them to contribute to the group's thinking on topics. Failing to do so would not only limit the relevance and effectiveness of the training, but it would surely prevent facilitators from taking advantage of the knowledge and experience that is brought by each group to the session. CCV wants instructors to understand that knowledge is created, not disseminated, through the group's interaction. In this way, instructors will see the benefits of promoting this type of communication in their own classes. CCV also learns a lot about what's on instructors' minds as they prepare to teach, and this in turn helps facilitators to better assess instructors' development needs both in the workshop and outside of it.

Generating Enthusiasm for the Coming Term

While excellent instructors come in all varieties, they usually share a few commonalities. For one thing, they have a solid grasp of their subject and can present it in a clear, simple, and articulate manner using active learning techniques to engage students. Also, most effective instructors have enthusiasm for their subject. When enthusiasm is combined with sensitivity to students' needs and a genuine concern for their development, it's a winning combination.

In Great Beginnings, facilitators try to acknowledge how instructors may be feeling as they approach their first semester at CCV. New instructors, like new students, may experience high levels of mental, physical, and emotional anxiety in facing the uncertainty of the classroom (Werner, 2003). By taking a proactive approach and encouraging instructors to reflect on the process of teaching and learning before they enter the classroom, facilitators hope to transform their fears into enthusiasm. In effect, they try to connect them to their original desire to teach.

Facilitators do a number of exercises in the Great Beginnings orientation. They introduce instructors to active learning strategies. They arrange them in small groups to solve classroom case studies, challenges that compel them to respond with creativity and collaboration. Once instructors learn how to design activities that engage students, facilitators introduce them to assessment. Feedback is important to the development of learners, and new instructors especially need to think about the ways they will give feedback and receive it. Finally, since it's essential for new instructors to experience a CCV class as students might experience it, CCV provides participants with the opportunity to shift perspectives and gain insight on what it's like to be on the "other side of the desk."

Model Exercise From Great Beginnings

The shift of perspectives begins with the very first exercise, an opportunity for instructors to think about their own educational experiences—who they are as learners and who they want to be as teachers. After brief introductions, facilitators ask instructors to think of a teacher who has had a profoundly positive impact on their lives. They are encouraged to envision this teacher and think about the behaviors that he or she used in the classroom and with students.

Participants in the workshop are asked to write their impressions, memories, and thoughts about the teacher they have in mind. After a few minutes of writing, instructors are provided with a worksheet titled Characteristics in Teaching (see Figure 10.2). They must check off the characteristics exemplified by the teacher they have in mind. This takes a few more minutes as instructors transition from their own choices in language to the phrases and definitions provided on the worksheet.

At this point, facilitators ask instructors to make a leap from the teachers they have in mind, the ones they're most familiar with, perhaps, to college teachers in general. Which of the characteristics on the worksheet are most important? What are the five most important things teachers have to be or do in the college classroom?

Once instructors have independently decided this, they are divided into small groups where their "mission" is to find agreement on the five most important characteristics for college teachers and then articulate and defend their choices to the larger group. Later, as the exercise is debriefed, it's clear that a lot of discussion and thinking happens in the small group. Instructors share their stories regarding the people who likely impacted their decision to become a teacher; they share their values around teaching and the five characteristics they believe are impor-

FIGURE 10.2
CHARACTERISTICS IN TEACHING

Think of a teacher who had a profoundly positive influence on you as a student. This could be someone from grammar or high school, or it could be a professor from your own postsecondary experience. From the following list, decide which characteristics your teacher exemplified and make an X next to those qualities.

My teacher . . .

☐ liked or was interested in students
☐ was organized and clear about expectations
☐ encouraged independence through showing students how to learn
☐ demonstrated love of subject and was enthusiastic
☐ was flexible and willing to change under certain circumstances
☐ was compassionate and encouraging
☐ made the material meaningful and relevant to students
☐ was fun-loving and humorous
☐ was knowledgeable about the subject
☐ valued students' ideas and was a good listener
☐ taught problem solving through encouraging students to think for themselves
☐ was expressive, conveyed genuine affection for all students
☐ was fair to all students, demonstrated integrity
☐ demonstrated excellent speaking skills and was able to keep students' attention
☐ was consistent in how he or she presented expectations and requirements
☐ inspired and/or challenged students
☐ was friendly and personable
☐ was energetic and dynamic

tant. In the process, all participants engage in critical and conceptual thinking. They move from the concrete experience of examining individual teachers to developing an abstract model for college teaching.

Although it might be easier to simply tell instructors what behaviors are most effective in the classroom, such an approach would hardly engage them. Asking participants about their own experiences as students, however, hooks them into the topic and activates the learning process. The exercise becomes a model for the kinds of active learning and critical thinking CCV wants to see in a classroom. Students need opportunities to move from the concrete to the abstract, to collaborate with others, and to construct new ways of thinking. This exercise can assist instructors in thinking about how to provide those opportunities on their own. When facilitators use the exercise to connect to Kolb's (1984) Experiential Learning Cycle or Gardner's (1983, 1993) Multiple Intelligences, instructors also better understand how learning style theory can be applied in the classroom.

Finally, this exercise reminds instructors why they teach or want to teach. It encourages them to locate the image of "teacher" in their minds and analyze it for effective behavior or characteristics. In the process, instructors confront the assumptions they have made about teaching and learning. Whose responsibility is it, for instance, to make a subject meaningful—the instructor's or the student's? If an instructor has envisioned teaching as a metaphor for something else—whether it be performer, coach, or midwife—how is that metaphor likely to sustain and constrain him or her? Questions such as these help instructors to be more purposeful about their goals for teaching in their first semester and beyond.

Teaching for Development: CCV's Instructor Handbook

Self-reflection is essential for the new instructor; it's where the orientation begins and often where it ends. In fact, according to a recent phenomenological research study, it's what new instructors are most engaged in when they begin teaching (Werner, 2003). However, teaching is also about the practical aspects of being in the classroom and navigating a great deal of turbulence or uncertainty. Without some attention to technique, new instructors can become lost in the experience and take their students with them. This is why CCV devotes time in Great Beginnings for demonstrating ways to use its instructor handbook.

The handbook provides information about CCV policies and its mission, vision, and values. It provides information about students—who they are and what their different needs might be. But the handbook also includes some valuable suggestions for, among other things, creating a syllabus, building community, using small groups, organizing content, designing assignments, relating to students, and evaluating writing.

Facilitators use the handbook to support several key strategies during the course of the orientation. Some of these strategies follow.

Emphasize the Use of Learning Objectives in Teaching a Course

Each semester instructors must develop their course descriptions, which provide students with a brief summary of the course, a list of essential learning objectives, the assigned text(s), the methods that will be used in teaching the course (including course requirements), the evaluation strategies, the grading criteria, and the attendance policy. While each part of the course description is critical for what it conveys to students, the list of essential learning objectives is, perhaps, the most important. Not only have the objectives been developed and approved through a college-wide process, but they focus on what a successful student should be able to do or know; therefore, they are essential in clarifying students' expectations about performance. In addition, they provide instructors with specific goals with which they can align their classroom activities and assignments.

To this end, facilitators show instructors a sample course description and planning matrix and discuss how they can use the learning objectives to frame the semester's curriculum. Instructors need to consider how their objectives connect to other elements of planning, such as class activities, student assessment, evaluation methods, and resources. This is vital since students are evaluated on the basis of how well they meet the objectives of their course. Thinking about how to teach while accommodating a wide variety of learning styles and reflecting on the pace and sequence of learning can go a long way toward establishing a supportive climate for student learning.

Reinforce the Principles of Good Teaching and Learning

These principles provide instructors with a framework for thinking about their work in the classroom before they enter it. After asking instructors to reflect on an excellent teacher in their lives and to determine what characteristics are most important in this regard, facilitators draw instructors' attention to the principles, which are prominently featured in the handbook. It's quite easy to make the connection, since many of the values espoused by instructors are also articulated in the principles. In addition, when assessment and evaluation is discussed, facilitators are careful to illustrate how students receive feedback from instructors and give it to them. At the end of every semester, students are asked to complete a feedback form on the instruction they received. Since both of these documents, the principles and the feedback form, articulate the college's expectations for instructors, it's vital that these are shared at the beginning of the semester.

Illustrate How Best Practices Can Be Used to Solve Various Classroom Challenges

Once instructors have discussed teaching at the abstract level, facilitators move to an exercise that compels them to apply their knowledge and skills in solving classroom case studies. Instructors are arranged in small groups, provided one "challenge," and encouraged to use the handbook as a resource.

The use of case scenarios allows facilitators to engage instructors in the real work of teaching, illustrate the importance of multiple perspectives, promote critical thinking, connect theory to practice, and enhance problem-solving skills. The following are just a few of the case study problems offered during the course of the orientation.

- You're an anatomy and physiology instructor who wants more discussion in the classroom. Students are so busy taking notes, they don't seem to think about what they're writing or what you're saying. How could you design a small-group activity to promote discussion? What other ways might you encourage more thoughtful and relevant discussion?

- You're preparing to teach American history for the first time. You love history, but you know what turns off undergrads—the idea that history is a dry compilation of names and dates. You think your passion for the subject will engage students, but how can you create exams that don't reduce everything to names and dates?

- You're teaching psychology online this semester. Students are communicating with you and each other on a frequent basis and entirely in writing. You're fairly comfortable with grading students' formal papers, but this is so much more than that. Some students approach their weekly postings with only casual regard for punctuation, and others are merely regurgitating material from their texts. What kinds of writing assignments might you design to get students thinking more critically or originally about the subject? And how might you establish some guidelines for their writing?

- You're teaching a management course for the first time this semester. You designed a final project assignment that is flexible, leaving students with plenty of opportunities for different approaches. A few days before the assignment is due, you develop a rubric to help you evaluate the projects. When the projects are submitted, however, you note with some alarm that two students have turned in work that is unlike the others. In fact, based upon your rubric, these students wouldn't receive any credit. To make matters worse, both projects technically follow the initial guidelines of your assignment. What might you do to resolve this problem? What are the issues? Would you make any changes the next time around? Why or why not?

What makes CCV's handbook so valuable is simple. It's not just targeted for instructors; it's drawn from them—their experience, their wisdom, and their ingenuity in the classroom. In doing so, it combines both the reflective and the practical; it relies on the premise that most instructors want to be the kind of teacher who inspires others.

Summary and Conclusions

The Great Beginnings orientation provides the foundation for instructor development efforts. By requiring all instructors who are new at CCV to attend, the college is able to ensure that the entire faculty has participated in exercises on the philosophy of teaching, student diversity, active learning, and assessment and evaluation. Coordinators, who work closely with instructors during the semester, can further emphasize and expand upon the lessons of Great Beginnings through informal conversations, site-based workshops, and one-on-one meetings. Feedback from the orientation has been so positive that many instructors and coordinators have suggested a follow-up workshop titled Great Beginnings II.

Of course, CCV is committed to providing opportunities for instructor development beyond Great Beginnings. Semiannual conferences and numerous trainings, both at the programmatic and course level, are offered to instructors. CCV has begun work on a pilot instructor mentor project that pairs veteran instructors with new instructors from the same field. These and other development opportunities are offered in order to improve student learning outcomes in academic programs, offer enhanced support and feedback for instructors, and create active, reflective, and responsive learning environments.

Several research studies begun in the 1990s document the trend toward hiring increasing numbers of part-time faculty at two-year institutions of higher education (Gappa & Leslie, 1993; Mahoney & Sallis, 1991; O'Banion & Associates, 1994). With 100% part-time faculty, CCV recognizes the critical necessity of supporting adjunct instructors. The life of the college depends on them. By focusing on instructors in their first semester, providing proactive high-quality training, encouraging reflective dialogue, and connecting instructors to each other and staff, CCV works to build the kinds of relationships that visibly support and enrich a teaching and learning institution.

References

Angelo, T. A., & Cross, K. P. (1994). *Classroom assessment techniques: A handbook for college teachers.* San Francisco, CA: Jossey-Bass.

Gappa, J. M., & Leslie, D. W. (1993). *The invisible faculty: Improving the status of part-timers in higher education.* San Francisco, CA: Jossey-Bass.

Gardner, H. (1983). *Frames of mind.* New York, NY: Basic Books.

Gardner, H. (1993). *Multiple intelligences: The theory in practice.* New York, NY: Basic Books.

Kolb, D. A. (1984). *Experiential learning: Experience as the source of learning and development.* Upper Saddle River, NJ: Prentice-Hall.

Mahoney, J., & Sallis, L. (Eds.). (1991). *Community, technical, and junior college statistical yearbook.* Washington, DC: National Center for Higher Education.

O'Banion, T. (1997). *Creating more learning-centered community colleges.* Mission Viejo, CA: League for Innovation in the Community College.

O'Banion, T., & Associates. (1994). *Teaching and learning in the community college.* Washington, DC: American Association of Community Colleges.

Vermont State Colleges. (2004). *Mission of the Vermont State Colleges system.* Waterbury, VT: Author. Retrieved July 21, 2004, from http://web.vsc.edu/visitors/82.html

Werner, R. (2003). *Making invisible voices visible: Reflections on learning to teach by new part-time community college instructors—a phenomenological study.* Unpublished doctoral dissertation, Capella University, Minneapolis, MN.

11 | THE RIO SALADO COLLEGE SYSTEM'S APPROACH TO STRATEGIC SUCCESS WITH ADJUNCT FACULTY

Hazel M. Davis, Laura Helminski, and Vernon C. Smith

Rio Salado College (also referred to as Rio) was established in 1978 as the sixth of ten Maricopa Community Colleges in Maricopa County, Arizona, the largest community college system in the nation, also known as MCCD. Conceived as a college without walls, Rio was designed as an institution that provided education to the underserved and unserved geographic areas of the county, unlike the traditional brick and mortar colleges that make up the remainder of MCCD. At its founding, part of its mandate from the MCCD Governing Board was that the college would operate primarily through the employment of adjunct faculty. Rio has been remarkably successful over the years with its use of adjunct faculty, and it was one of the colleges extensively profiled as a model in the 1995 publication *Strangers in Their Own Land* (Roueche, Roueche, & Milliron).

Since that time, the evolution of the college has continued, undergoing the transformation from a nontraditional institution serving a distance learning population through a variety of modalities and locations such as shopping centers, schools, and public buildings as well as on television, to serving those distant students in a primarily online environment. During the 2002–2003 academic year, approximately 24,000 students accounted for almost 48,000 duplicated enrollments, with 92% of those enrollments in the college's online courses. In fall

2003, the college had an enrollment of 10,162 full-time student equivalent (FTSE) and employed 28 permanent residential faculty and close to 850 adjunct faculty, of whom approximately 450 are online distance learning instructors teaching 263 distinct Internet courses.

The college has been markedly successful in recruiting and retaining adjunct faculty. In spring 2003, almost 80% of adjunct faculty had taught for the college for more than four semesters, and 35% for 13 semesters or more, with a turnover rate of less than 5% (Rio Salado College, 2003).

Most of the permanent residential faculty serve as faculty chairs, functioning as curriculum specialists and instructional leaders to the adjunct faculty who teach in their disciplines. Additionally, the college has 26 "starts" annually for over 90% of distance learning courses offered. This means that students can enroll in and begin a course at any time during the year, effectively doing away with the semester model and requiring the hiring of adjunct faculty year round. Adjunct faculty may have a single course section containing students who have up to four different start dates. Given this environment, it has been vitally important for the college to have a clear and deliberate approach to recruiting, supporting, and retaining the adjunct faculty who, by design, help the college to accomplish its mission and purposes through meeting the level of high expectations that the college imposes, and who will fit into the unique culture of a nontraditional institution.

How does Rio maintain quality—in recruitment, retention, and evaluation—in this environment? The college deliberately focuses considerable time and resources on support mechanisms for the operational aspects of teaching, so that adjunct faculty can spend more of their time on teaching and learning activities.

Synthesis of Related Literature

The literature on the use of adjunct faculty in institutions of higher education documents issues that Rio does not face. What are the myths and assumptions that may be holding back other community colleges in terms of how they can support adjunct faculty? It is important to understand the myths and assumptions about adjunct faculty in order to better understand how to work successfully with them. Certainly the utilization of adjunct faculty has increased in higher education and in community colleges in particular. Between 1976 and 1995, part-time faculty utilization increased by 91% (Clery, 1998). By the fall of 1998, higher education institutions in the United States employed 40% to 43% of their faculty ranks as part-timers (Leslie, 1998; Wilson, 2001). In 1999, only 35% of the faculty at public two-year colleges were employed full-time, compared with 59% at private four-year colleges or 70% at public four-year colleges (U.S. Department of Education, 2003). In higher education, then, it is clear that the utilization of adjunct faculty to teach more classes is a trend that is increasing at a rate likely to make it the common characteristic of many institutions, if that is not the case already.

A review of the literature reveals that the issues surrounding adjunct faculty have changed little over the past 20 years. Most of the literature can be placed into two arenas: the motivation for the utilization of adjunct faculty and the relationship between the employment of adjunct faculty and educational quality. Each arena presents opposing viewpoints with corresponding solutions to accompany the critical processes of recruitment, selection, evaluation, training, and retention of adjunct faculty.

The literature found in the motivational arena universally acknowledges the rapid growth of adjunct faculty but differs on the reasons behind decisions to employ them. It is clear that employment of adjunct faculty reflect larger global and economic trends toward cost-savings, especially in an environment of shrinking governmental resources at the federal and state levels in the United States. Adjunct faculty have been described as the abused "working poor," as "accidental faculty" (Gappa & Leslie, 1993), as "strangers," and as full-, half-, or part "mooners" (Roueche et al., 1995). The use of adjunct faculty has been viewed as de-professionalizing the faculty role, which then leads to the "de-skilling" and disempowerment of full-time faculty (Cohen & Brawer, 1982; Rhoades, 1998). Adjunct faculty also can be perceived as not being integrated into the community of scholars, and thus marginalized and less effective. A basic assumption in this school of thought is that an adjunct faculty member is either unable or unwilling to make the commitment or shoulder the responsibility needed for effective learning to take place.

The greater use of adjunct faculty is a clear marker or characteristic of the growing trend of academic capitalism, in which "educational actors" participate in market and market-like behavior, acting in very entrepreneurial ways (Slaughter & Leslie, 1997; Slaughter & Rhoades, in press). The use of adjunct faculty, especially from the managerial perspective, keeps costs down, provides more flexibility for educational institutions and, therefore, more agility in meeting market needs or demands. Given the ever-quickening pace of change and globalization, it is the practitioner who has the most current knowledge—especially in terms of technology. A practitioner is more likely to be found in business or industry than in the educational sector. Adjunct faculty who are practitioners bring real-world experience and practical application to the classroom, which have been shown to be critical elements in effective teaching and learning (Bransford, Brown, & Cocking, 1999).

Adjunct faculty, especially those teaching in the community college setting, are more likely to have been community college students themselves (Keim, 1989). While this is not especially surprising, since two-year colleges make up more than 42% of all higher education institutions in the United States (The Carnegie Foundation for the Advancement of Teaching, 2001), given the increasing diversity of today's student populations, adjunct faculty may be powerful role models for students because they have had similar life experiences.

Some of the literature addressing the issue of quality relating to the employment of adjunct faculty argues explicitly or implicitly that the use of adjunct faculty has an overall negative impact on the quality of higher education. This impact ranges from claims of the disintegration of the scholarly community to the de facto inflation of grades when an adjunct faculty, rather than a full-time faculty, is employed (Sonner, 2000). However, Roueche et al. (1995) noted that no significant study showed a difference in educational outcomes through the use of adjunct faculty.

Outside of these two mainstreams of research, some studies have begun to disaggregate and analyze the available data and to confirm or reject these commonly held mental models about adjunct faculty in the community college, including their levels of commitment and expectations for students (Freeland, 1998; Rifkin, 1998). Implications for practice are inherent from each perspective: to avoid using adjunct faculty where possible or at least to be very selective; alternatively, to invest in adjunct faculty in terms of support, professional development, and enhancement of their capabilities. And finally, there is the movement toward organizing, unionizing, and collective bargaining by adjunct faculty (Cason, Estep, & Hixson, 1999).

Given this background, how does an academic institution support adjunct faculty effectively in a nontraditional college like Rio so that they can concentrate on teaching? What barriers might exist in achieving the goal of having adjunct faculty contribute to quality teaching and learning?

The Rio Salado College Adjunct Faculty Model

Because of the unique faculty infrastructure at Rio, the training and support mechanisms offered along with the continuing opportunities for learning ensure that the college hires, supports, and maintains a truly outstanding cadre of adjunct faculty. The college takes care of operational needs so that adjunct faculty can focus on teaching. Having a deliberate model for recruiting, supporting and retaining adjunct faculty gives the leadership of Rio a framework for discussion, as well as a systemic view for planning and improving at all levels the strategies that the college uses with its adjunct faculty. Rio employs the metaphor of the old-fashioned milk bottle in which the cream rises to the top to exemplify its adjunct faculty model. Because of its heavy reliance on adjunct faculty Rio has placed extensive resources into its processes involving adjunct faculty. The richness provided in the mix stems from the support strategies, inclusion and collaboration strategies, and strategies for higher expectations that are practiced by the college regarding adjunct faculty. The adjunct faculty members, or cream, rise to the top because there is enough richness provided by the support infrastructure that is suspended in the "milk" below (see Figure 11.1).

FIGURE 11.1
ADJUNCT FACULTY MODEL

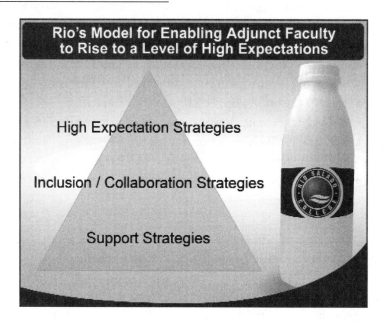

Maslow's hierarchy exemplifies a similar model for achieving peak performance (see Figure 11.2). Once humans satisfy their basic physiological and safety needs, esteem and social needs will require fulfillment. With a sufficiently perceived level of satisfaction for esteem and social needs, the ability to concentrate on the fulfillment of self-actualization becomes possible. Rio has deliberately designed strategies that address the specific cluster of needs that correspond to the strata of Maslow's hierarchy. Support strategies have been developed over time to address physiological and safety needs of adjunct faculty. The social and esteem needs of adjunct faculty have been met by specific inclusion and collaboration strategies. Finally, strategies that promote high expectations of performance from adjunct faculty can help them fulfill self-actualization needs. While there is, of course, individual variation from faculty member to faculty member, on the whole these strategies seem to address the real needs of the adjunct faculty as a group working in the distance learning context at Rio.

FIGURE 11.2
MASLOW'S HIERARCHY AND RIO'S MODEL

The Rio infrastructure is unusual in that it has been systematically designed to support adjunct faculty as well as full-time faculty. This makes sense in a nontraditional institution where most of the courses are taught by adjunct faculty. The college utilizes a "one course, many sections" model whereby exactly the same course is taught in all distance learning sections of a discipline, regardless of who is teaching the course. The course content and materials are initially developed by the faculty chair, or by a developer hired by the chair, who then works closely with the chair to develop content that meets the course competencies. For quality assurance, the course is taught by the developer the first time it is offered. Thereafter, the same course would be taught by any faculty member hired to teach in the discipline. Resultantly, there is no difference whether the course is taught by adjunct or full-time faculty, and the rigorous development process and infrastructure assure the quality of the course.

The college's comprehensive mechanisms that are in place to hire, support, and mentor approximately 800 adjunct faculty through a systemic grid of support strategies, inclusion and collaboration strategies, and high expectation strategies, have been very successful. An adjunct faculty motivation survey, designed to elicit the impact of the college's attention to adjunct faculty support, had 85% of respondents (N = 189) agreeing or strongly agreeing that that the college pays ongoing, deliberate attention to providing support for its adjunct faculty (Rio Salado College, 2003).

Support Strategies

At Rio, several different departments are involved in providing support strategies to the college's adjunct faculty. Each of these departments provides specific services to ensure that a comprehensive support infrastructure is in place.

The staffing of all courses is centralized in the Department of Faculty Services. The managers of this department work closely with the faculty chairs to place instructors in close to 3,000 sections each semester. Recruitment of adjunct faculty is an ongoing process throughout the year because classes start every two weeks in the distance learning format, and because of the just-in-time training needs of business and industry. The department recruits instructors through advertisements placed in local newspapers, targeted organizations, networks of current faculty, and referrals from the community. Additionally, in 2002, the adjunct faculty application form was placed online and has elicited an overwhelming response, with an average of 80 applications being received weekly. Once a candidate is interviewed and approved, personnel information and course interest selections are entered into the faculty information system database.

As with residential faculty, newly-hired adjunct faculty must meet MCCD hiring requirements in order to teach. For returning adjunct faculty, the faculty services team, working closely with the faculty chairs, reviews performance data, student and faculty evaluations, and teaching preferences in order to match the faculty with appropriate courses and modes of delivery.

Rio's technology helpdesk plays an important role in supporting distance students and the college's employees, including adjunct faculty, by providing generalized technology support. The technology helpdesk team is available seven days a week. Students and employees can receive help in person, over the Internet, or on the telephone.

In addition to the technology helpdesk, Rio has in place an instructional helpdesk, designed specifically to assist distance learning adjunct faculty and students with questions about such issues as distance learning formats and course materials. The instructional helpdesk personnel are experienced distance learning adjunct faculty members who are able to facilitate solutions to issues and to provide general or specialized assistance to adjunct faculty and to students. The team offers training for new distance learning instructors, administrative assistance, consulting, and limited technical assistance, while acting as a liaison between the faculty chairs and adjunct faculty. A database is maintained to track resolution of faculty and student requests and issues. The instructional helpdesk team is responsible for the Please Call program, whereby distance learning students are contacted during the first three weeks of class to ensure that they are proceeding well. This mechanism further supports adjunct faculty by contributing to the retention of the students in their classes.

Rio's course support department produces and distributes introductory materials to distance learning students and adjunct faculty, such as welcome letters and instructions on how to access their courses, as well as providing adjunct faculty with supplies and discipline-specific materials needed to teach their courses. Course support receives mailed or faxed assignments from students and schedules them for delivery to adjunct faculty via the college's courier service.

Couriers have the responsibility of delivering and picking up all materials necessary to ensure that instructional and learning activities are carried out with little or no disruption. The courier service operates six days a week, and provides pick-ups and deliveries between all college sites, adjunct faculty homes, and any location where college activity is conducted throughout Maricopa County in Arizona (where Rio's headquarters is located), thus providing a valuable link between the college and its instructors. Each month, the couriers average 2,100 deliveries, driving approximately 15,500 miles.

The college's library services are tailored to accommodate a distance learning student and adjunct faculty population. Adjunct faculty may request books and audio-visual materials from the library's collection either by telephone or online, and these materials are then delivered to their homes by courier. The library's web site provides access to a substantial collection of full-text electronic databases, including journal, magazine, and newspaper articles, images, encyclopedias, ERIC and e-books, available via a proxy server to adjunct faculty and registered students from any computer with Internet access. An introduction and orientation to Rio's library services, in CD or video format, is provided to all adjunct faculty when they first sign up to teach for the college. The college librarians provide reference services via email, live chat, telephone, and in person to accommodate the needs of distance learning students and faculty.

Tutoring services also are available in telephone, live chat, email, and in-person modalities, enabling adjunct faculty to readily refer students for tutoring in the format that best suits the students' needs. Additionally, the college's counselors provide personal and career counseling in-person, by telephone, and by email, again providing a service that adjunct faculty can readily refer to their students.

Inclusion/Collaboration Strategies

The inclusion of adjunct faculty in the work of teaching and learning and in the curriculum discussions at a college underlies the issue of the quality of that institution. This is based on several assumptions, including the fact that it is difficult, if not impossible, to know of the pedagogical emphases of the institution if adjunct faculty are not available for inclusion in faculty meetings and faculty development opportunities where the full-time faculty frequently have these discussions. Nonetheless, adjunct faculty generally are not included because of their lack of availability, rather than their lack of desire. However, as the literature demonstrates, there is a concern about the ongoing quality of instruction for students when adjunct faculty are not involved in conversations with full-time faculty. Another issue arising from the literature is the notion that part-time faculty are only partly committed because they are not present. This assumption can also be based on their availability and not on their motivation or interest. The difficulty of involving part-time employees is a reality in most workplace situations, and not just in higher education.

However, this does not mean that inclusion and collaboration cannot be increased. The adjunct faculty motivation survey showed 61% of the adjunct faculty agreeing or strongly agreeing that ongoing deliberate attention is paid to including adjunct faculty in department-level discussions and decisions at Rio (Rio Salado College, 2003). This is a significant percentage, given the issues that surfaced in the literature review regarding claims of disintegration of the scholarly community with the hiring of adjunct faculty.

At Rio, strategies for inclusion and collaboration between full-time and adjunct faculty are accomplished in two primary work areas: discipline support and professional development support.

Discipline Support: The Work of Faculty Chairs

There is generally one full-time residential faculty member per academic discipline or department who also serves as the faculty chair, a practice that supports and aligns with the college's focused vision and mission statements. As faculty chairs, these residential faculty's primary responsibilities are to communicate with, mentor, and support the adjunct faculty in their disciplines. This expands the role of the department chair at traditional campuses. Rio faculty chairs focus on six major areas of responsibility: 1) teaching; 2) instructional leadership, which includes training adjunct faculty, participating in college assessment work, monitoring retention, monitoring and improving outcomes in their disciplines, and participating in educational conferences; 3) curriculum development, including data-driven improvements, textbook selection, and teaching and learning strategies (including implementing e-learning and accelerated pedagogies into the curriculum); 4) department management, including supervising and evaluating adjunct faculty; 5) communication with students; and 6) participating on college and district committees, college-wide system projects or initiatives, and work as staff development trainers. They lead discipline dialogues as well as department curriculum and assessment teams. Rio's faculty chairs do not have to spend much time on such operations or logistics as recruiting and hiring adjunct faculty, textbook orders, or classroom reservations since the college has support systems that perform these functions. Thus, they can focus on instructional, pedagogical, and curricular leadership.

Professional Development Support: The Work of the Faculty Development Coordinator and the Faculty Development Committee

Formal faculty development activities for Rio adjunct faculty are coordinated and supported by the faculty development coordinator, the faculty development committee, the faculty chairs, and the instructional helpdesk team. These well-attended activities include ongoing new faculty orientations, biannual All-Faculty Learning Experiences (fall and spring) with Discipline Dialogue sessions, ongoing Distance Learning Faculty Successful Start workshops, Effective Distance Learning Instruction workshops, and Online Professional Development workshops. Additionally, there is an in-person fall and spring schedule of professional development workshops offered by Rio and by the MCCD district-level Maricopa Center for Learning and Instruction. The all-faculty learning experiences frequently highlight national speakers on current educational topics and trends. The adjunct faculty often have the opportunity to hear the same speakers that are brought to the college on a regular basis to provide new learning for faculty, administrators, and staff. Adjunct faculty receive continuing education units for participating in many of these activities. Each year, the college recognizes outstanding adjunct faculty in the areas of teaching and contributions to assessment. The award-winning faculty members are selected by the faculty chairs, with input from student evaluations and their own observations, and are honored in the presence of their peers at the all-faculty learning experience.

Technology training, provided by the instructional helpdesk, is ongoing in order to prepare adjunct faculty to teach online classes or to utilize the voicemail system. Professional growth funds are available through the MCCD district office for conferences and workshops, with the faculty services department handling the application process for adjunct faculty. Seventy-two percent of respondents to the human, physical, and financial resources adjunct faculty survey agreed or strongly agreed that the adjunct faculty development workshops and training provided them with needed information and support to function effectively in their positions, while 73% reported that the opportunities for professional growth and development offered by the college were sufficient (Rio Salado College, 2000).

College-level communication with adjunct faculty occurs through the *Inside Rio* newsletter, the online faculty support page, and faculty development mailings. However, the primary communication is from the discipline faculty chair and includes mailings, email, teleconferences, online conference folders, and in-person meetings. In the human, physical, and financial resources adjunct faculty survey, 80% of respondents agreed or strongly agreed that their faculty chair shared with them the information they needed to do their job. Survey data were extremely positive, showing that 95% of adjunct faculty felt that their work helped Rio accomplish its mission, while 84% of respondents reported that they felt respected on the job, with 80% indicating that they felt valued for the quality of the work they did. Additionally, 84% agreed or strongly agreed that the workload for their position was fair, while 79% agreed or strongly agreed that they had access to the resources needed to do their job well (Rio Salado College, 2000).

Faculty Support Page

The primary tool for communicating with adjunct faculty to help facilitate their work is the online faculty support page. This web site was carefully designed by the faculty chairs to provide adjunct faculty with immediate access to the tools, resources, and support services that they need on an ongoing and updated basis. From the many links on this site, adjunct faculty can access updated rosters, schedule teleconferences, review competency rubrics, access all of the support services provided by the college, schedule an in-person training, or take an online faculty development workshop for which they can earn continuing education units.

High Expectation Strategies

Rio's culture is based on the principles and practices of continuous improvement. This includes a major focus on customer service, with meeting (indeed, exceeding) the customers' expectations being the primary goal. Faculty and administration work together continuously, serving on teams to analyze processes, improve them, and monitor the results. The strategy of having published "expectations statements" focuses attention on the commitment of all Rio employees to customer service. In 2002, college expectations for adjunct faculty were developed by the faculty chairs, and then each faculty chair worked with her or his adjunct faculty to develop a department expectations statement. These statements clarified expected working behaviors and emphasized how faculty, students, and the college would work together for effective teaching and learning to occur. Adjunct faculty involvement in the development of these statements was crucial since they are the frontline employees working with the students and they can assess what is realistic and what is necessary. The value of published expectations statements for adjunct faculty, for faculty chairs, and for the college is that they contribute to the ability of these stakeholders to communicate more clearly and to work together more productively. In the adjunct faculty motivation survey, 77% of the adjunct faculty agreed or strongly agreed that ongoing, deliberate attention is paid to agreement on consistently high expectations for distance learning instruction at Rio, as well as to meeting these expectations (Rio Salado College, 2003).

Department expectations for adjunct faculty usually include statements of response time and requirements for grading and feedback. Since these statements are developed by the faculty chair in collaboration with the adjunct faculty, there are many important discussions that lead to the final statement, and there is an increased sense of inclusion and value among the adjunct faculty.

Summary and Conclusions

The results of Rio's adjunct faculty strategies are impressive, as indicated by survey data. An integrity and practices survey of adjunct faculty conducted in 2001 (N = 227) demonstrated that an overwhelming 95% of Rio adjunct faculty felt that their work helped the college accomplish its mission, while well over 80% reported that they felt respected and valued for the quality of their work at Rio. Turnover rate is less than 5%. In the adjunct faculty motivation survey, respondents awarded high praise to the support services and activities that allow them to focus on quality teaching and learning at the college. Such innovations as the instructional helpdesk, technology helpdesk, courier services, and discipline dialogues all scored above 4.0 on a 5.0 point scale. Examples of feedback comments included:

- "Whenever I have a problem, I know right where to go to get help."
- "Anything I ever need or ask for I receive immediately from Rio."
- "I can focus on the class, not paper work."
- "Rio is innovative and has great respect for adjunct faculty."
- "Rio allows adjunct faculty to teach the course . . . and be attentive to the students without having to focus on administrative tasks. This allows us to do what we really love and want to do."

During Rio's successful 10-year accreditation renewal by the Higher Learning Commission of the North Central Association in 2002, the college's implementation of its Plan for Assessment and Improvement of Student Learning was named a best practice by the accreditation team for involving adjunct faculty in assessment work. This recognition is evidence of the success of its deliberate and structured adjunct faculty model.

Conclusions about Rio's emphasis on support can be readily drawn through specific comments from the adjunct faculty motivation survey. One adjunct faculty member wrote:

Whenever I have needed assistance with problems of any type, response has been speedy and professional. Staff at Rio have always approached my concerns in a professional manner and no problem or question is considered silly or unimportant. As a result of the great service support staff provide, I am able to concentrate on facilitating learning and the Internet classroom experience. . . . Students become my focus, not technology.

And finally: "You think of improvements before I do."

References

Bransford, J. D., Brown, A. L., & Cocking, R. R. (Eds.). (1999). *How people learn: Brain, mind, experience, and school.* Washington, DC: National Academy Press.

The Carnegie Foundation for the Advancement of Teaching. (2001). *The Carnegie classification of institutions of higher education.* Menlo Park, CA: Author. Retrieved September 5, 2003, from http://www.carnegiefoundation.org/Classification/down loads/2000_Classification.pdf

Cason, F., Estep, J., & Hixson, K. (1999, February). Part-timers unite! Adjunct professors struggle for equal rights. *New Art Examiner, 26*(5), 38–42.

Clery, S. (1998). *Faculty in academe.* Washington, DC: National Education Association, Office of Higher Education. (ERIC Document Reproduction Service No. ED423740)

Cohen, A. M., & Brawer, F. B. (1982). *The American community college.* San Francisco, CA: Jossey-Bass.

Freeland, R. (1998). *Adjunct faculty in the community college.* Unpublished manuscript. (ERIC Document Reproduction Service No. ED424899)

Gappa, J. M., & Leslie, D. W. (1993). *The invisible faculty: Improving the status of part-timers in higher education.* San Francisco, CA: Jossey-Bass.

Keim, M. C. (1989). Two-year college faculty: A research update. *Community College Review, 17*(3), 34–43.

Leslie, D. W. (1998). *Part-time, adjunct, and temporary faculty: The new majority?* (Report of the Sloan conference on part-time and adjunct faculty). (ERIC Document Reproduction Service No. ED422771)

Rhoades, G. (1998). *Managed professionals: Unionized faculty and restructuring academic labor.* Albany, NY: State University of New York Press.

Rifkin, T. (1998). *Differences between the professional attitudes of full- and part-time faculty.* Paper presented at the American Association of Community Colleges Convention, Miami, FL. (ERIC Document Reproduction Service No. ED417783)

Rio Salado College. (2000). *Human, physical, and financial resources survey—adjunct faculty.* Unpublished raw data.

Rio Salado College. (2001). *Integrity and practice survey—adjunct faculty.* Unpublished raw data.

Rio Salado College. (2003). *Adjunct faculty motivation survey.* Unpublished raw data.

Roueche, J. E., Roueche, S. D., & Milliron, M. D. (1995). *Strangers in their own land: Part-time faculty in American community colleges.* Washington DC: Community College Press.

Slaughter, S., & Leslie, L. L. (1997). *Academic capitalism: Politics, policies, and the entrepreneurial university.* Baltimore, MD: Johns Hopkins University Press.

Slaughter, S., & Rhoades, G. (in press). *Academic capitalism in the new economy.* Baltimore, MD: Johns Hopkins University Press.

Sonner, B. S. (2000, September/October). A is for adjunct: Examining grade inflation in higher education. *Journal of Education for Business, 76*(1), 5–8.

U.S. Department of Education, National Center for Education Statistics. (2003). *Digest of education statistics, 2002.* Retrieved September 12, 2003, from http://nces.ed.gov/programs/digest/d02/list_tables3.asp#c3

Wilson, R. (2001, May 4). Proportion of part-time faculty members leveled off from 1992 to 1998, data show. *Chronicle of Higher Education,* p. A14.

12 | A Case Study of the Online Adjunct Training Environment at Santa Fe Community College

Richard L. Wagoner

For the past 25 years scholars and practitioners alike have all agreed that to better integrate and retain adjunct faculty into the culture of postsecondary institutions those faculty must be offered the opportunity to grow professionally, to interact meaningfully with their full-time peers, and to contribute to the academic life of the institution (Gappa & Leslie, 1993; Greive & Worden, 2000; Leslie, 1998; Parsons, 1980; Roueche, Roueche, & Milliron, 1995). While these recommendations have been made consistently, little has been done to make them a reality. The problem of fully integrating part-time faculty into the academic life of an institution is particularly crucial for community colleges for two reasons. First, community colleges employ, and therefore rely on, a significantly higher percentage of adjunct faculty than any other segment in postsecondary education, 64% of all community college faculty in 1997 (American Association of Community Colleges [AACC], 2000). And, because they are teaching institutions, community colleges must be focused on the instructional ability and quality, not just the content knowledge, of all faculty members (Cohen & Brawer, 2003). Because part-time faculty are not regularly present at a campus, a commonly cited difficulty to better integrating them into a college's culture is the lack of a convenient time and place for orientation and training or interaction between full-

and part-time faculty members. With the advent of computer network technology, it has been suggested that problems presented by time and place can be neutralized by asynchronous sessions for training and faculty interactions (Greive & Worden, 2000). This chapter will analyze a computer- based support and professional development program at one Florida community college to evaluate its effectiveness and its potential as a model to help all community colleges better integrate part-time faculty into the academic lives of their campuses.

A second goal for the chapter is to offer a critique of the use of part-time faculty at community colleges based on the assumption that part-timers are institutionalized as a highly managed (Rhoades, 1998) workforce as a result of the globalization of the community college (Levin, 2001). Ultimately, the intention of the chapter is to present viable programs that can better support and integrate part-time faculty, while simultaneously offering a theoretical perspective that increases understanding of adjunct faculty.

Literature Review

Given the dual purposes of the chapter, two strains of literature will be addressed, beginning with a discussion of part-time faculty—their positions at community colleges and best practices for their use, followed by a discussion of how the ideology of the new economy has fixed itself in the organizational thinking of community colleges, and how that change in thinking, in part, has lead to the globalization of community colleges (Levin, 2001).

The use of part-time faculty in community colleges is pervasive; 64% of faculty at all community colleges were designated as part-time in 1997 (AACC, 2000). Many popular critics take this aggregate data as proof there is a crisis that must be solved, whether that crisis one of undue exploitation of part-timers (Dubson, 2001), the erosion of academic quality (Benjamin, 2002), or both (Karabell, 1998) tends to be the only question. Others (Biles & Tuckman, 1986; Gappa & Leslie, 1993, 1997; Roueche et al., 1995) argue that the use of part-time faculty is essential for community colleges to meet their multiple missions and to offer open access and flexibility for the community. While this second group of scholars recognizes that there are problems with the use of part-timers, they advocate reform of the system with the use of best practices focusing on recruiting, hiring, and retention policies, working conditions, and integration of part-time faculty into the culture of the college. While it can be debated whether there is a crisis, most scholars agree that there are two differing justifications for the use of part-time faculty in community colleges.

Jacobs (1998) points out that, traditionally, part-time faculty were used to increase the prestige of institutions. Part-timers were most often visiting scholars, artists in residence, skilled professionals or technical workers, or distinguished citizens. In all these cases, the part-time faculty member brought skills, abilities, and talents to the institution that were not possessed by the regular faculty. This traditional use of part-time faculty continues today and is considered a good and valued practice. Generally, the majority of these part-timers either have full-time employment outside the college or are retired.

Many scholars (Benjamin, 1998; Biles & Tuckman, 1986; Gappa & Leslie, 1993; Jacobs, 1998) have suggested the rising problem of part-time faculty in higher education does not center on this traditional use of part-timers, but on their use as convenient and expedient means to lower costs and increase flexibility for institutions (Gappa & Leslie, 1997; Rhoades, 1996; Roueche et al., 1995). This more recent trend in the use of part-time faculty has increased dramatically as the percentage of part-time faculty has grown over the last 30 years. These part-time faculty members are not viewed in the same positive light as traditional part-timers. They are frequently viewed as less skilled and trained than full-time faculty; the quality of their instruction and their dedication to the institution is questioned.

These two differing uses of part-time faculty are the source of tensions. The first relates to the intention of administrators at community colleges: Are part-time faculty employed because they increase the quality of the faculty and program offerings, thus increasing quality and access for students, or are they employed primarily as financial expedients, which may bolster the bottom line but not the institution's mission? Assuming that both of these motivations can exist at one institution simultaneously leads to the second problem. Benjamin (1998) demonstrates that differing clusters of part-timers at community colleges have significant differences in several areas including annual income, educational attainment, and teaching practices. These clusters are the vocationally oriented cluster—a group of disciplines from areas that are not traditional academic subjects, where much valued experience and training can be acquired outside of the academy— and the liberal arts cluster—a group of disciplines traditionally found in the academy, with faculty that have acquired their experience inside the academy. This distinction is important. The traditional use of part-time faculty hinges on their bringing abilities and talents not found at an institution, which members of the vocationally oriented cluster do. Members of the liberal arts cluster, however, possess skills that are already abundant on community college campuses. Therefore, the second source of tension has to do with bifurcation, not only between full- and part-time faculty, but between the differing clusters of part-timers themselves. While part-time faculty have always been used in vocational programs, a large part of the increase of part-timers in recent years has come from the traditional liberal art fields. A recent study (Wagoner, Metcalfe, & Olaore, in press) indicates that this expanded use of liberal arts part-timers is indicative of administration seeking increased flexibility in programs, increased control of faculty, and increased fiscal savings, elements that resemble the ideology of the new economy and globalization.

The new economy, with its emphasis on lean and flexible organizations capable of exploiting the demands of a constantly changing marketplace, is a prime factor in the process Levin (2001) has described as globalizing the community college. For Levin, globalization is a scholarly concern that is both a concept and a process. Conceptually it represents a compression of both time and place. As a process it "intensifies social and political relationships and heightens economic competition" (p. x). Globalization then is both an environmental, or external, force influencing community college response, and, once internalized by members of the community college, a cultural belief and internal force about the goals and mission of the community college.

A movement toward the marketplace and the neoliberal state characterizes the process of globalization. That is, during the last 20 years, community colleges have been influenced by both private businesses and the national government. This influence has led community colleges to emphasize workforce training and state economic competitiveness while adopting an orientation closely resembling new economy business models. The effect is to emphasize productivity, efficiency, and the comodification of education and training.

Levin (2001) suggests that while there is a wide array of definitions about what globalization is, there is consensus on how it shapes organizations. It drives the production process for organizations to increase profits. For nonprofit organizations the drive to increase profits is manifested as an emphasis on increasing flexibility and efficiencies. Part-time faculty are at the heart of this drive toward efficiency for community colleges. Adjunct faculty are inexpensive and allow management tremendous flexibility to respond to consumer/market demands. All part-time faculty, both those from the vocational fields and from the liberal arts fields, have become central to the mission and success of the globalized community college.

The literature demonstrates that when considering part-time faculty at community colleges it is crucial to employ more than one perspective to develop a more nuanced appreciation of their use. A functionalist perspective (Gappa & Leslie, 1993; Roueche et al., 1995) gives a clear picture of the use, status, and environment of part-timers at community colleges. A critical perspective (Levin, 2001; Rhoades, 1996) offers an alternative to the functionalist. That is, the best practices advocated from the functionalist perspective are essential for trying to improve the position of part-timers at community colleges; therefore, any analysis of training programs must consider these best practices. It is also important to explore how a critical perspective illuminates the possible motivations behind these programs, which allows for a deeper understanding of the organizations themselves and, perhaps, problem areas the functionalist perspective might miss.

Method

Given the importance of the functionalist and critical perspectives to this study both will be incorporated into its analysis. A functionalist perspective highlights two central questions. First, what evidence is there to suggest that the program under study is more effective for integrating adjunct faculty into a campus's culture? And, if it is more effective, how can such a technology-based program be established at other community colleges? If the program has been successful in its attempt to better train and integrate part-time faculty, those findings are immediately valuable for practitioners as they evaluate support available for part-timers and plan for changes on their campuses.

The research is a case study (Yin, 1994) of an online support and training program at one Florida community college that received a multiyear grant from the Fund for the Improvement of Postsecondary Education (FIPSE) to develop such a program. The program at Santa Fe Community College (SFCC) in Gainesville, Florida, is known as the On-line Adjunct Training Environment (OATE) and is intended to "give adjuncts the information they need and a means of connecting with their fellow faculty, departments, and institutions."

The case relies primarily on document analysis, with an emphasis on the online artifacts made available by the program. The universal resource locators (URLs or web addresses) of all web sites are included so those interested in the program can view and analyze it for themselves. The data also includes one semi-structured personal interview with a principal of the program. The interview offers a means of triangulation to confirm findings from the online documents and to clarify any questions the document analysis produced. While the case presents an explanation of the OATE program, the researcher is most interested in examining the challenges faced by the program, how those challenges were or were not met, the relative success of the program, and how other colleges might implement similar programs to improve the training and integration of their adjunct faculty. The challenges faced by the program are important from both a functionalist and critical perspective. From the functionalist perspective, challenges offer valuable insight for planning to any college considering such a program. From the critical perspective, the challenges also reveal how globalization and the new economy might influence decisions and practices for similar programs at other colleges.

The case was selected purposively because SFCC received federal grant funds to develop its program. The rationale was that this federally funded project would have the resources to better meet its goals than most ad hoc programs. One other assumption influenced the selection of the case: Resources, both human and financial, must be employed if a college is to improve its training and integration of part-time faculty. Therefore, the OATE program was selected in the belief that it would show significant positive benefits, which, in turn, would justify the cost of implementing such a program.

Findings

The program at SFCC, originally known as the On-line Adjunct Training Environment (OATE), intends to "give adjuncts the information they need and a means of connecting with their fellow faculty, departments, and institutions." The FIPSE grant for the OATE project began in 1997 and continued through 2001. During the course of the project its name changed and is now known as the Online Faculty Teaching Excellence Network (OFTEN). The website and data source for analysis is http://inst.sfcc.edu/~often/.

The project sought "to integrate adjuncts into the college as true faculty, rather than as a marginal group" by providing access to the Internet, email, and discussion boards. This access was intended to overcome the obstacles that make face-to-face training difficult, if not impossible, for part-time faculty. Integration would be accomplished by allowing adjuncts to interact with other faculty, both full- and part-time, using email and discussion boards. Beyond this informal interaction the grant also included funds for more formal mentoring to occur between full- and part-time faculty in each department. Training would be accomplished using a web site that provided all the information a new faculty member would need to succeed at SFCC. During the grant, all part-time faculty offices were equipped with a computer wired to the campus network, and training was available to all part-time faculty to ensure that they were able to use the technology made available to them. Each of these elements was intended to lead to the fulfillment of the goals of the project: 1) to enhance the teaching effectiveness of adjunct faculty, 2) to increase the sense of college community, and 3) to improve adjuncts' ability to integrate technology into their courses. It is clear from the goals that one of the benefits of an online program is that by participating in it part-timers build skills that can translate directly to the classroom. And, the training itself models teaching and learning in an online environment. The first two goals are focused on traditional teaching values of community colleges. The third goal, by privileging technology as an instructional method, is tied to the ideology of the new economy and globalization which values the power and efficiency of computers to accomplish what traditionally have been labor- intensive activities.

The depository of all important information, the project's web site is the primary accomplishment for the program. The OFTEN web site has links to the following departments/divisions: English, creative arts and humanities, natural science, social science, and mathematics. A sample of the English department's home page is shown in Figure 12.1.

From this sample, it is clear that the information available is comprehensive. All departments use a similar template. The institutional information is identical from site to site, and each department has information for its particular courses. Each department's web page was reviewed and found to contain clear and concise information that

FIGURE 12.1
ENGLISH DEPARTMENT HOME PAGE ON THE OFTEN WEB SITE

Department	SFCC Information	Pedagogy
• Departmental Website	• SFCC Website	• ENC 1101
• English Faculty Photos	• SFCC Faculty Handbook	• ENC 1102
	• SFCC Student Profile	• ENC 2301
	• SFCC Human Resources	• Teaching and Learning Links
	• SFCC Adjunct Faculty Site	

Faculty/Student Services	Rules and Regulations	Technologies
• Faculty Services	• Gordon Rule	• Computers
• Student Services	• English Faculty Requirements	• Phones
	• English Department Student Policies	• Library
		• Audio-Visual

would be valuable to any faculty member. In terms of having a convenient and comprehensive method of conveying essential information to part-time faculty, OFTEN is quite successful.

Because of this initial success other support services and campus representation is now available to part-time faculty. There is an adjunct faculty web page that offers links to all of these services (http://inst.sfcc.edu/~adjfac/). This web page and all of the programs on it are a direct result of the initial OATE program. Like the OFTEN web site, the adjunct faculty web site contains links to high-quality information specifically for part-timers, including an adjunct newsletter. Beyond the information the page offers, there are links to the President's Committee for Part-time Faculty Affairs, the adjunct advocate—a support person for part-timers—and the two adjunct faculty representatives on the faculty senate. The six-member Committee for Part-time Faculty Affairs includes the two adjunct faculty members of the faculty senate and the adjunct advocate. The link to the committee allows part-timers to access the minutes from the committee's monthly meetings, which offers adjuncts tangible evidence that their concerns are heard and that they have representation in campus affairs.

Given the availability of these committee documents, the minutes from two recent meetings (May and June of 2003, http://inst.santafe.cc.fl.us/~adjfac/minutes.html) were analyzed to get a sense of the issues the committee addresses and what those issues might indicate for part-time faculty at SFCC. Several issues demonstrate the position for adjuncts is changing. Most interestingly, there is a new designation for some adjuncts. This group, identified by the acronym DROP, is paid full-time salaries. It is unclear if DROP faculty are full-time instructors without long-term contracts or if they are part-timers who are paid at the same rate per course as full-time faculty. In either case, DROP faculty have gained a status many part-timers would treasure. All faculty, including part-timers, did receive a 2% raise in pay for the next school year. This indicates that part-time faculty were included with full-timers for these negotiations, a sign that part-timers are better integrated at SFCC than they sometimes are at other community colleges. Long-term parking permits are also available for adjuncts, which eliminates the need to get a new permit each term.

All of the developments above demonstrate that SFCC considers adjuncts central to its mission and that part-timers have had their position on the campus improve since the FIPSE grant began. The fact that many of these benefits were not originally intended as a part of the FIPSE grant demonstrates that a program such as this can have unimagined positive results if it is begun. All of these developments are a solid model for other colleges to emulate, but what about the challenges faced during the grant?

In general, there were two challenging areas. One is evidenced in the name change the program underwent. The other was financial. Simply comparing the two different names for the program illuminates the first challenge. Originally, the program was known as the On-line Adjunct Training Environment (OATE). During the project it was changed to the Online Faculty Teaching Excellence Network (OFTEN). With the name change adjuncts appear to no longer be a separate class of instructor, but included with all faculty. At one level it is possible to see this as evidence that adjuncts have been integrated into the faculty as a whole, accomplishing the one faculty advocated by Gappa and Leslie (1997) and no longer requiring the designation as adjunct. In the interview the researcher found that this was not the case. Both full-time and part-time faculty objected to the OATE designation, and both groups wanted it changed, not necessarily because they saw themselves as one faculty. Members of the full-time faculty felt that adjuncts were receiving special treatment and wanted the training as well. Many adjuncts were opposed to the adjunct label. In the end, OATE became OFTEN. Not because full-time and part-time faculty embraced each other as one, but because each had their own motivations to eliminate the term "adjunct."

The financial difficulties for the project came after the grant ended. According to the interviewee, there has been little or no money available to maintain the project and, as such, continuing work on the project is an act of good will. At one level this can be explained by the success of the original grant project, the resulting strengthening of SFCC's web presence, and the development of its information technology (IT) department. Since this project was SFCC's first foray into the online environment, it has resulted in new departments on campus that deal with all technology programs. This interpretation demonstrates positive benefits for the college as a whole, but also shows that there is no longer a budget for a dedicated program to meet part-timer's needs. That is, there is now a strong IT department at the college, but no one in the department is assigned specifically to maintain the adjunct project. Any work done to continue the adjunct project must be done on a volunteer basis. Which is to say little work is done. In terms of technology training there is no problem because all campus members are able to receive training from the IT department. But in terms of the mentoring done for part-timers it is quite problematical. If there is no incentive for a faculty member to mentor part-timers, they do not receive mentoring. As mentoring was one of the key elements of the original program, without it one of the goals of the project can no longer be realized.

These two primary challenges stem from the FIPSE grant itself, but what of the other areas that have come about because of the success of the grant—the adjunct web site and the programs it encompasses? As there was evidence of positive changes from the minutes of May and June 2003 President's Committee for Part-time Faculty Affairs meetings, there is also evidence that many of the problems surrounding adjuncts nationwide still exist at SFCC. The minutes from the May and June 2003 meetings demonstrate that there are still problems with the status of part-timers and the various resources available to them, which ultimately affects their morale.

The first issue concerns parking permits. While parking permits are available to part-time faculty for an entire year, not just the current session, they are only issued after part-timers sign a legal document concerning the status of their employment. Committee minutes from the May 2003 meeting indicate that in order to receive a parking permit part-timers "must fill out a form which specifically states that this does not imply an expectancy of full-time employment." Even for something as trivial (perhaps parking at any college should not be categorized as trivial) as a parking pass adjuncts are not only reminded of their marginal status, but they also must sign a document affirming it. Murphy (2000) insists that colleges must be concerned about clearly defining the legal status of part-time faculty, but in this case, such a document for a parking pass probably does more to alienate part-time faculty than it does to protect the college.

If parking is a concern for most adjuncts, the availability of office space is constantly listed as a priority. As mentioned above all, departments at SFCC do have offices available for part-time faculty, but the May 2003 minutes indicate that this resource is overburdened.

> [A committee member] raised a problem of etiquette in adjunct offices. Since there are no written guidelines for adjunct offices, she recommends a list of expectations, like an adjunct office ten commandments. They would include: faculty must share desks and computers; don't leave stuff on the desk; each is entitled to a drawer. . . .

Office space for part-timers is considered essential if they are to feel valued and a part of their college. According to the interviewee every department does have adjunct offices, but some can have as many as 12 adjuncts in one office. Given these limited resources it is understandable that some part-timers would try to monopolize them, leading to the need for etiquette guidelines. It is interesting that this type of competition for limited resources causes part-timers to compete with one another, to see other part-timers in their own departments as competitors, not colleagues.

This potential schism in the ranks of part-timers is also evident in a point about the representatives to the faculty senate also from the May minutes. "Adjunct senate representatives: there is a concern that the representatives are not reporting to their constituents. [A committee member] will ask the representatives to send information from the senate meetings to [the webmaster] to put on the web site." Representation in the faculty senate is a great thing, but if adjuncts are not aware of what is happening then the value of the representatives is at best symbolic, and the question of whose interests are being served—all adjuncts or only those on the senate—must also be asked. Beyond that, if the web site is not accessed by all part-timers, its value is limited. In this case alternate methods of dissemination should be considered, or the web site, which is maintained by the college IT department, not staff dedicated to adjunct faculty issues, can be seen as an inexpensive means for the administration to show support for part-timers while dedicating few resources to such support.

Financial resources are also a problem when considering the new faculty raise. The minutes from the June committee meeting contain an observation from one of the members indicating that a 2% raise for both full- and part-time faculty "destroys equity since lower salaries get lower actual raises. The new adjunct rate is $548 per credit hour." As discussed earlier, it is heartening that part-timers were included with the full-time faculty in the negotiation of the new pay raise, but several problems do rise from the situation. The first concerns the tension between that which is fair and that which is equitable. It is fair that all faculty members received the same percentage pay increase, but as indicated by the meeting minutes, the identical percentage of pay increase actually amplifies the disparity between part-time and full-time faculty. The second problem stems from the first: $548 per credit hour for part-time faculty is considerably lower than the equivalent pay for full-timers. A larger percentage increase to part-time faculty would have helped to decrease the difference in pay, which would clearly make part-timers feel they are valued and that their position is improving. If part-timers feel more valued perhaps it would increase their willingness and availability to more fully participate in the academic life of the college.

The low participation rate of part-timers in the President's Committee for Part-time Faculty Affairs is another area of contention illuminated by the June meeting minutes. "Committee membership: We urge everyone who is interested to come to meetings. We are continually disappointed that so few adjuncts take the time to come." Even with the efforts of the OFTEN program, part-timers are still unavailable. Perhaps they are too busy to attend such meetings—in that case it is wonderful that they have the minutes available on the Internet. But, if part-timers feel undercompensated and not valued by the college, they may choose to not participate because of their perceived lack of status. In either case the traditional problem of part-timers not actively participating in the intellectual life of the campus continues.

The final point from the June meeting minutes indicates that part-timers might be dissatisfied with their positions as opposed to being too busy to participate in campus life. "[The adjunct advocate] will include a pep-talk message [in the next newsletter] to adjuncts to remind them that titles and salaries are not indicators of their value." This is a great sentiment, and clearly the OATE/OFTEN program has made a great effort to increase the skills, quality of instruction, and standing of SFCC's part-time faculty. But it will take more than a pep-talk to convince adjuncts that titles and salaries are not indicators of value. That is, titles and salaries have always been a prime indicator of value both in business and in education, and, if part-timers at SFCC feel that they are not valued, it will take a determined effort by the administration of the college to improve the position of part-timers. In all of these examples a lack of resources lies at the heart of the problems. In order for part-time faculty to become better trained and integrated into a campus, resources must be available. If the only motivation to use part-timers is a financial one, adequate resources will not be made available, and part-timers will remain marginal.

Discussion

The findings demonstrate that OFTEN has had a strong, positive result on the SFCC campus. The program has not only met its original goals of increasing teaching effectiveness and integrating part-time faculty into the campus community, but its initial success has also led to increased programs and representation for part-timers. From a functionalist perspective, the value of such a program cannot be disputed. A critical perspective allows practitioners and scholars to understand how the challenges the program has faced illuminate concerns that have implications beyond the development of such a program.

The original intent of adjunct support and training has changed, making the program available to all faculty, not just part-timers. Not a planned extension of the program, this change was due primarily to the dissatisfaction of both full- and part-time faculty. The change demonstrates how the mindset and practices of the new economy has influenced community colleges. In this case different segments of the faculty labor market compete for scarce resources, which can cause tension between full- and part-time faculty, leading to further separation of the two groups, rather than integration.

Financing is a key factor for the program. Without the FIPSE grant money the program would not have been realized. Now, however, financial support for the program has shifted to the institution. As a direct result of this shift the SFCC technology department now maintains the web site and computer literacy training, but all other mentoring and incentives for part-timers ended with the FIPSE grant money. Therefore, the overall needs of part-timers become marginal as the original intention and source of funding for the program changes.

Both the functionalist and critical perspectives indicate that a change needs to come in the status and support of part-timers if their increased use is to be sustained. In that sense, the SFCC program shows positive signs. Their status has changed—they are included in the technology budget, they have direct representation in administration, and technological resources are made available to them similar to full-timers. Once again, however, resources and finances are still a divisive issue in three areas. First, the program has come to include full-time as well as part-time faculty, so whatever limited resources are expended are there to serve more than the part-timers. Salary and office space are the other two examples of inequity. Part-timers still have much less resources allocated to their needs in these two areas. Globalization theory indicates that efficiency is the root of the increased use of adjuncts; if that is true, then one would expect to see a pattern of little financial resources being expended by colleges, which is true at SFCC in these three areas.

There is one other result of the program that has increased demands on part-time faculty while not increasing the amount of resources expended for them. The OATE/OFTEN program has increased the administrative demands on some part-time faculty, including two members on the faculty senate, three members on the president's advisory committee, and an adjunct newsletter. In these cases, part-timers might be seeking to gain the status of regular faculty, but they are still not equal to full-timers. Smith (2001) argues that part-timers may take on such extra duties in the belief that doing so will increase their status at the institution and strengthen their bids for a full-time position.

The OATE/OFTEN program shows positive signs from the functionalist perspective—there is more support and training on these campus then there was before the program, and that is good for all constituencies of the college. But from a new economic perspective the program can be seen as supporting in various ways the continued exploitation of part-timers, or certainly the continuing bifurcation of the community college faculty labor force.

Summary and Conclusions

This study offers evidence of the value of incorporating technological means for integrating and training part-time faculty, while at the same time indicating that support and training costs associated with adjuncts should be viewed as investments in the well-being of the learning community of a college, not as costs diminishing the bottom-line efficiencies of the use of part-time faculty. SFCC has demonstrated positive outcomes for the part-time faculty it serves. While much of the initial evidence is anecdotal, part-time faculty at SFCC have stated that they feel better prepared to teach and that they are doing a better job. Such feelings certainly ensure that attitudes and relationships have improved on campus.

Evidence suggests that many colleges avoid such training for part-timers because it is perceived as a cost and not an investment. This is supported by data from the 1999 National Study of Postsecondary Faculty. In this study 72.4% of full-time faculty at public two-year institutions reported having internal training available for professional development, while only 24.7% of part-time faculty at similar institutions have such training available (U.S. Department of Education, 2001). If community colleges are going to continue their high use of part-time faculty some investment must be made in their training and integration so colleges can continue to meet the needs of communities well into the 21st century. By making such training available, colleges acknowledge that part-time faculty are valuable human resources and as such deserve to be invested in for the long-term success of the college. When these investments are not made, particularly if the decision against them is a financial one, college administrations show they are more interested in economic efficiency—a position similar in view to the corporate world now dominated by the new economy, not the traditional mission of community colleges, which values human relations and the development of all members of the community.

References

American Association of Community Colleges. (2000). *National profile of community colleges: Trends and statistics 1997–1998.* Washington, DC: Community College Press.

Benjamin, E. (1998). Variations in the characteristics of part-time faculty by general fields of instruction and research. In D. W. Leslie (Ed.), *New directions for higher education: No. 104. The growing use of part-time faculty: Understanding causes and effects* (pp. 45–59). San Francisco, CA: Jossey-Bass.

Benjamin, E. (2002, Fall). How over-reliance on contingent appointments diminishes faculty involvement in student learning. *Peer Review, 5*(1), 4–10.

Biles, G. E., & Tuckman, H. P. (1986). *Part-time faculty personnel management policies.* New York, NY: American Council on Education/Macmillan.

Cohen, A. M., & Brawer, F. B. (2003). *The American community college* (4th ed.). San Francisco, CA: Jossey-Bass.

Dubson, M. (Ed.). (2001). *Ghosts in the classroom: Stories of college adjunct faculty—and the price we all pay.* Boston, MA: Camel's Back Books.

Gappa, J. M., & Leslie, D. W. (1993). *The invisible faculty: Improving the status of part-timers in higher education.* San Francisco: Jossey-Bass.

Gappa, J. M., & Leslie, D. W. (1997). *Two faculties or one? The conundrum of part-timers in a bifurcated work force* (New Pathways Working Paper Series, Inquiry No. 6). Washington, DC: American Association for Higher Education.

Greive, D. E., & Worden, C. A. (Eds.). (2000). *Managing adjunct and part-time faculty for the new millennium.* Elyria, OH: Info-Tec.

Jacobs, F. (1998). Using part-time faculty more effectively. In D. W. Leslie (Ed.), *New directions for higher education: No. 104. The growing use of part-time faculty: Understanding causes and effects* (pp. 81–88). San Francisco, CA: Jossey-Bass.

Karabell, Z. (1998). Adjuncts and community colleges. In *What's college for? The struggle to define American higher education* (pp. 191–211). New York, NY: Basic Books.

Leslie, D. W. (1998). New directions for research, policy development, and practice. In D. W. Leslie (Ed.), *New directions for higher education: No. 104. The growing use of part-time faculty: Understanding causes and effects* (pp. 95–100). San Francisco, CA: Jossey-Bass.

Levin, J. S. (2001). *Globalizing the community college: Strategies for change in the twenty-first century.* New York, NY: Palgrave.

Murphy, W. (2000). Legal issues in higher education for adjunct faculty. In D. E. Greive & C. A. Worden (Eds.), *Managing adjunct and part-time faculty for the new millennium* (pp. 119–141). Elyria, OH: Info-Tec.

Parsons, M. H. (1980). Future directions: Eight steps to parity for part-time faculty. In M. H. Parsons (Ed.), *New directions for community colleges: No. 30. Using part-time faculty effectively* (pp. 85–88). San Francisco, CA: Jossey-Bass.

Rhoades, G. (1996, November/December). Reorganizing the faculty workforce for flexibility: Part-time professional labor. *Journal of Higher Education, 67*(6), 626–659.

Rhoades, G. (1998). *Managed professionals: Unionized faculty and restructuring academic labor.* Albany, NY: State University of New York Press.

Roueche, J. E., Roueche, S. D., & Milliron, M. D. (1995). *Strangers in their own land: Part-time faculty in American community colleges.* Washington, DC: Community College Press.

Smith, V. (2001). *Crossing the great divide: Worker risk and opportunity in the new economy.* Ithaca, NY: ILR Press.

U.S. Department of Education, National Center for Education Statistics. (2001). *Institutional policies and practices: Findings from the 1999 National Study of Postsecondary Faculty, institutional survey.* Washington, DC: Author. Retrieved July 22, 2004, from http://nces.ed.gov/pubs2001/2001201.pdf

Wagoner, R. L., Metcalfe, A., & Olaore, I. (in press). Fiscal reality and academic quality: Part-time faculty and the challenge to organizational culture at community colleges. *Community College Journal of Research and Practice.*

Yin, R. K. (1994). *Case study research: Design and methods* (2nd ed.). Thousand Oaks, CA: Sage

13 | Implications and Recommendations for Recruiting, Supporting, and Retaining Adjunct Faculty

Desna L. Wallin

This book began with the caveat that in dealing with part-time faculty it is important to recognize that one size does not fit all. There is great diversity in purpose, in preparation, in motivation, and in pedagogy among part-timers. But, as anyone who has spent time in higher education knows, there is also great diversity in purpose, preparation, motivation, and pedagogy among full-time faculty.

Part-time faculty are indeed here to stay and their ranks will likely grow in the years ahead. They are absolutely necessary if community colleges are to fulfill their teaching mission. Part-time faculty bring with them an understanding of the community in which they live and work. They bring to the classroom real-world, real-life experience that no amount of book learning can replace.

Most research indicates that not only do they bring experience to the classroom, but they are also successful in communicating that experience to students. Their demographics are similar to their full-time colleagues and they are equally successful in the classroom. And much like the majority of their students, they are adult learners who bring a variety of life experience to the classroom. They tend to be problem-centered learners rather than subject-centered learners. They are more likely to be motivated by internal rather than external factors. They want to believe that they are bringing value to the lives of their students. These are considerations that the leaders charged with organizing faculty development activities would be well-advised to understand and build upon.

Nearly every author commented in some way on the importance of careful screening of potential adjunct faculty. In practice, the recruiting and hiring of part-time faculty is too often conducted with a cavalier attitude, knowing that the institution is not making a long-term commitment to part-time faculty. And yet, collectively, the institution is making an immense commitment to a corps of part-time faculty who will influence the lives, the attitudes, and the job prospects of thousands of students. The part-time faculty literally have the reputation of the college in their hands. Johnson County Community College (Chapters 5 and 7) and Brookhaven College (Chapter 6) have both demonstrated a commitment to hire the right people and spend the time and resources necessary to orient and support them. They provide excellent models for other colleges seeking to hire and support quality part-time faculty. Indian River Community College (Chapter 8) has similarly developed a comprehensive professional development program that is built upon the real needs of part-time faculty. It gives more than mere lip service to recognizing the contributions of part-time faculty and celebrating their successes. It takes the time necessary to determine their needs and then builds the program around those needs. Equally important, the college makes the effort to recognize publicly the accomplishments and contributions of their part-time faculty.

Leaders who are committed to providing professional development opportunities for adjunct faculty have long been frustrated by the increasingly difficult challenge of bringing faculty together in one place at one time. The growth of the Internet and attendant technologies have provided new avenues for bringing professional development to harried and hectic lives. There is no need to "tune in" at a particular time; there is no need to dress up and drive to a central location. Instead, learning can be asynchronous and accessed on the schedule of the adjunct, not the schedule of college administrators.

Particularly in budget-challenged times, it is difficult for a single college to provide comprehensive support to part-time faculty. Forming a consortium of like-minded colleges to share in the development and delivery of part-time faculty support may be the answer. The California consortium that comprises 4faculty.org provides an excellent example of what can be done (Chapter 9).

Those who are best at utilizing the possibilities of distance learning are those who have worked in an online instructional environment long enough to recognize both the benefits and the drawbacks of online learning. The Community College of Vermont (Chapter 10) and Rio Salado College (Chapter 11) are stellar examples of colleges that provide successful online coursework for their students. They have extended that expertise to their large cadre of part-time faculty. When the majority of faculty are adjunct, their needs and concerns are heeded.

Santa Fe Community College (Chapter 12) has shown "the value of incorporating technological means for integrating and training part-time faculty," as well as another point that is echoed throughout the book: Providing support and training for part-time faculty is not a cost that diminishes the bottom line. Rather, it is an investment in the well-being of the college and its students.

Recommendations

The contributors to this volume provided a wealth of ideas that can be adapted to the needs of colleges of all sizes, geographic locations, and philosophies. The overarching recommendation from all the contributors would seem to be that college leadership needs to be absolutely certain that part-time faculty are valued and recognized for their contributions to the college. Some specific recommendations follow.

- Design problem-based professional development activities. Use case studies and/or classroom vignettes to illustrate real issues that faculty face in the classroom.
- Knowing that part-time faculty are more likely to be motivated internally than externally, do everything possible to provide an environment that reinforces their value to the organization and their belief that they are doing something worthwhile with their time and effort in the classroom.

- Provide the same basic access to materials, supplies, and equipment that full-time faculty take for granted. Copying services, computer access, and technical support are essential.
- Provide options for professional development. Consider both traditional and online delivery systems to meet the variety of schedules and needs.
- Operate with high expectations. Give a clear set of expectations and evaluate against that standard.
- Provide models of course syllabi, classroom management information, and textbook supplements and teachers' guides.
- Provide access to a part-time faculty handbook that gives basic policy information as well as types and locations of services.
- Take the time to provide a strong orientation to the college, its mission and philosophy, and the values of the institution.
- Consider the possibility of developing a consortium of colleges to provide professional development opportunities for part-time faculty through traditional regional meetings or more easily accessible online training.
- Communicate! Communicate! Communicate! Be creative in how you reach part-time faculty with timely and appropriate information about their classes, college activities, and college issues. Use electronic communication and provide part-time faculty with a college email address.

As community colleges continue to experience growth in numbers amid diminishing fiscal resources, part-time faculty will play an increasingly important role in meeting the instructional needs of students. Leaders will become even more aware of the centrality of the part-time faculty to the success of the teaching mission of the college. They will be able to more easily justify the resources necessary to invest in part-time faculty. Only then will institutions be able to consistently and successfully recruit, support, and retain great teachers for America's community colleges.

Index